Praise for *Everyone Included*

'Driven by her clear enthusiasm, informed by her own ... ... tion that no-one should have to leave their identity at the door on their way into work, Helen's book is a lively and accessible guide to both the theory and the practice of introducing belonging to the workplace as the next step on from traditional D&I initiatives. Free of headache-inducing management-consultancy buzzwords, it steers the reader through the process from initial board presentations to the granular details of drafting job descriptions to attract a genuinely diverse talent pool.'

David Whincup, Partner, Head of Labor and Employment Practice,
Squire Patton Boggs (UK) LLP

'The aim of nurturing genuine diversity and inclusion in the workplace is perhaps the number one challenge for organisational leaders in the 21st century. *Everyone Included* is an invaluable guide to why this agenda matters and offers a wealth of practical advice to those trying to deliver it in the real world.'

Paul Jenkins, Chief Executive, The Tavistock and Portman
NHS Foundation Trust

'Building a culture of belonging can help transform organisations. This book is a straightforward, practical guide for how you can create a culture of belonging in your organisation.'

Jig Ramji, Group Head of Talent, London Stock Exchange Group

'Written in Helen's inimitable no-nonsense style, this inspirational guide cuts through the jargon, and challenges traditional mindsets to think beyond inclusion for some to belonging for all, which is what the world needs right now.'

Karen Mosely, Managing Director, HLM Architects

'This book is a roller coaster ride that is definitely worth any discomfort you may feel as you allow it to disrupt traditional views of what it means to properly belong. Good leaders will like it. Great leaders will inevitably feel compelled to act on Helen's ground-breaking straight thinking on what it means to be fully human at work.'

Julie Stokes OBE, Executive Coach and
Consultant Clinical Psychologist, The Preston Associates

'Helen May has a remarkable ability to synthesize complex and uncomfortable concepts in a way that's encouraging and inspiring. *Everyone Included* is a must-read for all genuinely engaged and inclusive leaders.'

Shannon Cassidy, Founder and CEO, Bridge Between, Inc.; Podcast Host;
author Grounded in Gratitude and V.I.B.E.

Pearson

At Pearson, we have a simple mission: to help people make more of their lives through learning.

We combine innovative learning technology with trusted content and educational expertise to provide engaging and effective learning experiences that serve people wherever and whenever they are learning.

From classroom to boardroom, our curriculum materials, digital learning tools and testing programmes help to educate millions of people worldwide – more than any other private enterprise.

Every day our work helps learning flourish, and wherever learning flourishes, so do people.

To learn more, please visit us at **www.pearson.com/uk**

Everyone Included

Improve belonging, diversity and inclusion in your team

Helen May

Pearson

Harlow, England • London • New York • Boston • San Francisco • Toronto • Sydney
Dubai • Singapore • Hong Kong • Tokyo • Seoul • Taipei • New Delhi
Cape Town • São Paulo • Mexico City • Madrid • Amsterdam • Munich • Paris • Milan

PEARSON EDUCATION LIMITED
KAO Two
KAO Park
Harlow CM17 9NA
United Kingdom
Tel: +44 (0) 1279 623623
Web: www.pearson.com/uk

First edition published 2022 (print and electronic)

ISBN: 978-1-292-34260-3 (print)
      978-1-292-34261-0 (PDF)
      978-1-292-34262-7 (ePub)

British Library Cataloguing-in-Publication Data
A catalogue record for the print edition is available from the British Library

Library of Congress Cataloging-in-Publication Data
A catalogue record for the printed edition is available from the Library of Congress

10 9 8 7 6 5 4 3 2 1
25 24 23 22 21

Cover design by Rogue Four Design

Print edition typeset in 10/14 Charter ITC Pro by Straive
Printed by Ashford Colour Press Ltd, Gosport

NOTE THAT ANY PAGE CROSS REFERENCES REFER TO THE PRINT EDITION

Contents

About the author   vii

Publisher's acknowledgements   ix

Introduction   xi

Key terms you need to know   xv

Part 1 The need for belonging   1

1. Why belonging is key to D&I initiatives   3

2. The Five Principles of Belonging   29

Part 2 How to create a sense of belonging   51

3. Carry out the Belonging Audit   53

4. Build your Belonging Plan   67

5. Get buy-in from the organisation   93

6. Put your Belonging Plan into action   107

7. Help your employees to thrive at work   131

Part 3 How to embed the culture of belonging   149

8. Keep the change going   151

9. It's down to you   165

Index   175

Contents

About the author

Helen has worked in Leadership, Talent & Culture for almost 25 years, holding senior corporate leadership positions before moving into consulting and setting up the diversity and inclusion business, Belonging@ Work®. Through her research, writing and leadership of global programmes, Helen has established herself as a strong thought leader and visionary in the diversity and leadership space. She also coaches private neurodivergent clients and advises organisations on how to maximise the unique talents of those who think differently.

Having been diagnosed with ADHD as an adult herself, Helen set up the community interest company 'Diverse Futures' which provides further education, apprenticeship and mentoring support for neurodivergent 16–25 year olds.

Publisher's acknowledgements

8 International Journal of Environmental Research and Public Health: Roberts JD, Mandic S, Fryer CS, Brachman ML, Ray R, Between Privilege and Oppression: An Intersectional Analysis of Active Transportation Experiences Among Washington D.C. Area Youth. *Intl. Journal of Environ Res Public Health.* 2019 Apr 12:16 (8):1313. doi: 10.3390/ijerph16081313. PMID: 31013698; PMCID: PMC6518066; **12 World Economic Forum:** World Economic Forum's annual convention DAVOS in January 2020; **13 Dow Jones and Company, Inc.:** Dieter Holger (2019), The Business Care for more Diversity, *The Wall Street Journal.* Retrieved from https://www.wsj.com/articles/the-business-case-for-more-diversity-11572091200; **19 Berrett-Koehler Publishers:** Charles H. Vogel, The art of community; **21 Alfred Adler**: Alfred Adler "Individual Psychology" 1926; **23–24 Accenture:** Accenture report 'Getting to Equal 2020: The Hidden Value of Culture Makers'; **34 Ann Tenbrunsel:** Quoted by Ann Tenbrunsel; **36 Mary T. Lathrap:** 'Judge Softly' Mary T. Lathrap, 1895; **38 Pat Wadors:** Pat Wadors (2016), then Vice President of Global Talent Organisation at LinkedIn, wrote in a *Harvard Business Review* article; **39 Bruce Sewell:** Quoted by Bruce Sewell; **40 Plato:** Quoted by Plato; **45 Simon Sinek:** Quoted by Simon Sinek; **46 Ari Kopoulos:** Quoted by Ari Kopoulos; **69 GoDaddy:** The statements above with that that of the domain registrar and web-hosting company GoDaddy; **75 Abadesi Osunsade:** Quoted by Abadesi Osunsade; **106 Association for Information Systems:** Adapted from Mendelow, A. L., "Environmental Scanning--The Impact of the Stakeholder

Publisher's acknowledgements

Concept" (1981). ICIS 1981 Proceedings. 20; **109 Bloomsbury Publishing:** Kirsty Bashforth describes in her book "Culture Shift: A Practical Guide to Managing Organisational Culture"; **125 NeuroLeadership Institute:** David Rock, SCARF: a brain-based model for collaborating with and influencing others, 2008 *NeuroLeadership Journal*; **126 Gallup Inc.:** Robert Sutton and Ben Wigert, "More Harm Than Good: The Truth About Performance Reviews", Gallup Inc. Retrieved from https://www.gallup.com/workplace/249332/harm-good-truth-performance-reviews.aspx; **133 Business in the Community:** BITC, Mental Health at Work, 2019. Retrieved from https://www2.deloitte.com/content/dam/Deloitte/uk/Documents/consultancy/deloitte-uk-mental-health-and-employers.pdf; **143 Victor Emil Frankl:** Quoted by Victor Emil Frankl; **146 Jillian Richardson:** Quoted by Jillian Richardson; **157 JOHN WILEY AND SONS INCORPORATED:**McMillan, D.W., & Chavis, D.M. (1986). Sense of community: A definition and theory. *Journal of Community Psychology*, 14, 6–23; **158 JOHN WILEY AND SONS INCORPORATED:** Adapted from Speer P, McMillan D. Validation of a brief sense of community scale: Confirmation of the principal theory of sense of community. *Journal of Community Psychology*. 2008; 36(1):61–73; **158 Andrea Rasca:** Quoted by Andrea Rasca; **160 Harry Levinson:** Quoted by Harry Levinson; **166 Brene Brown:** Quoted by Brene Brown; **169 Hany Shoukry:** Shoukry 'Coaching for Social Change'; **171 Brian Bi:** Forbes article, Brian Bi, former software engineer at Google, writes of how he believes we are transitioning from the Age of Information to the Age of Reckoning.

Introduction

What this book is about

In the increasingly divided, volatile and often perplexing world we are living in today, organisations are realising that, in order to protect the well-being and maximise the potential of their number one asset, their people, traditional approaches to diversity and inclusion (D&I) need a rethink. In this book, I will show you how shifting the focus to building a culture of belonging is the solution that will transform organisations, improve the lives of employees and create agile environments fit to adapt to challenges organisations are facing today and in an unpredictable future. A culture of belonging is going to be absolutely critical to business continuity. The evolution of organisations will require the individual employee to take centre stage, within a space where psychological safety is high, everyone feels included and the unique talents of all are maximised.

Belonging is an innate, human need as critical as our need for food, water and shelter. It has never been more important for us to find a sense of belonging in the world, to find a refuge in the middle of a chaotic environment. Inclusion is not enough. The act of being included does not necessarily mean that the individual feels accepted. These feelings do not support well-being, therefore impacting the individual's potential to be connected to the organisation. This disconnection impacts engagement and performance, creating organisational cultures where only certain groups of employees will thrive. Focusing on distinct, marginalised groups as traditional D&I programmes have done is not enough and has largely failed (or, at best, progress has been painfully slow).

The perception and nature of identity is evolving, with younger generations refusing to be put into convenient boxes. The slow progress to date is by no means a reflection on the passionate professionals who inhabit the space, but rather a frustrating inability to navigate organisational structures, leadership and business priorities to ensure D&I is a top priority on the organisational agenda.

In this book, I will introduce the concept of the organisation as a community, the principles of which underpin a sense of belonging for *everybody*. Creating a belonging culture places acceptance of individual identity and collective purpose within a shared community, as the core value at the heart of all people practices and processes. Our life at work impacts so much more than the time we spend there. It impacts well-being, security, self-esteem and overall life satisfaction. One of the most significant and influential groups of which we are a part, a sense of belonging, or not, at work has far-reaching consequences beyond organisational structures.

This book is not a D&I 101, so I won't be outlining the necessary regulatory and governance practices that have, in the large part, become the norm. I won't be covering solutions for each potentially marginalised group and I will not be outlining practices to increase minority representation. I won't wax lyrical about the commercial benefits of D&I, then provide tick boxes purported to make it happen. This book puts people before process, human experience before numeric targets and protection of well-being before results. This way, organisations will take responsibility for and contribute significantly to the good health and happiness of their employees. The results and financial gain will follow organically.

So, I am encouraging you to tear up the old manual and consider why and how a culture of belonging is critical to your organisation's future success.

Who this book is for

This book is designed to meet the needs of organisations and teams of all sizes. Its practical approach will be useful for:

- CEOs or senior leadership teams
- HR directors
- D&I specialists
- Well-being specialists
- Team or function leaders
- SME business owners.

How to use this book

This book guides you through the practical steps of building, implementing and embedding a belonging culture in your organisation. At each step, I will provide rationale and implementable actions to support you through the journey. It is also a personal journey, whoever you are, as understanding the concept of belonging can help you to understand yourself better, as well as those around you. Throughout the book, there are activities for you to do which will give you personal insights, improve your resilience and help you to build more successful, meaningful relationships in all areas of your life.

Part 1 will build understanding of the rationale behind this approach and guidance for looking at where you are now. This includes:

- why traditional D&I initiatives are failing and how belonging bridges the performance gap
- how the demographics in organisations and the nature of identity is evolving
- the Five Principles of Belonging built on the foundation of the organisation as a community
- a step-by-step guide to doing a Belonging Audit upon which to build the business case.

Part 2 introduces your step-by-step guide for developing and implementing a programme that lays the foundation for inclusion and belonging in your team/organisation. This includes:

- a framework for building your Belonging Plan
- how to build the business case, get commitment from decision makers and engage stakeholders
- how to implement your plan
- how to leverage belonging to support well-being.

Part 3 will focus on how you can measure progress as well as embed and sustain a belonging culture for now and the future that includes:

- how the belonging culture evolves over time and how you can extend the sense of community
- how your well-being and self-care are critical for feeling a sense of belonging, as well as creating it for others
- the wider belonging movement and why I am optimistic about the future.

This book is your complete guide to creating teams and organisations that focus on a culture of belonging where *everyone* is included and everyone can thrive.

Some ideas may be too radical for your organisation and some you may not agree with. That is OK. I would simply ask you to read the whole book and then think about where you can start, what you can do right now, today; when it comes to belonging, the smallest of changes can make a world of difference.

Enjoy the journey, I am grateful for your interest and I truly hope you find inspiration along the way.

Key terms you need to know

D&I vs belonging at work

I am sure you are well aware of what D&I is, but I think it is important to make a clear distinction between this and belonging. Your Belonging Plan is going to look very different from the traditional D&I one.

D&I is frequently described using the saying, 'Diversity is being invited to the party, inclusion is being asked to dance.' But D&I doesn't go far enough. What if I dance differently from others? What if I would prefer not to dance? What if I don't like the way people dance here? What if I think we could be dancing in a different way? Can we change the music? And, actually, why are we dancing? Inclusion infers that one group holds the power to include another group ('Would you like to dance?'). Often, the included group is expected to conform in response ('This is how we dance here'). D&I initiatives rarely consider the experiences of employees at an individual level. While many organisations focus on the importance of 'shared purpose' in creating employee engagement, most fail to consider creating meaning and sense of purpose at an individual level – which is how real emotional connectivity develops.

Belonging at work is the unique experience each employee feels relating to their liking, connection with and understanding of the organisation, culture and team. Belonging is driven by a feeling of positive regard, acceptance and social connectivity. It gives meaning and purpose to the work they do, underpinning motivation and effort. A sense of belonging supports physical and psychological health and is, therefore, fundamental to positive well-being and performance.

Equality vs equity

We are all familiar with the concept of equality, but, ironically, treating people equally is always going to disadvantage some employees. In order to decide on the parameters for equality, there has to be a certain benchmark and this is problematic for many reasons. Equality assumes one size fits all, but that can simply never be the case as some individuals and groups have very specific challenges that impact their ability to perform at their best. A more suitable goal in this context may be equity – the organisation enables and maximises the talent of every employee, by ensuring that they have all that they need to meet their needs. The diagram below demonstrates, in a simple way, how individuals should be given what they need to ensure they have the same opportunity as others to meet their goals.

Equality means that everyone gets the same, while equity means that people get what they need. It is an important distinction, as D&I has traditionally led with equality while belonging emphasises the need for equity.

To be very clear, equity does *not* mean that anyone gets unfair advantage over anyone else – it doesn't mean, as some critics say, that progress is enabled for some based on who they are and not their capability. Equity in the work-place means that everyone has the chance to maximise their talents. It means ensuring there is a diverse workforce by considering how the organisation truly connects with and provides opportunity for a broad range of people – from attraction and recruitment, through to development and career progression.

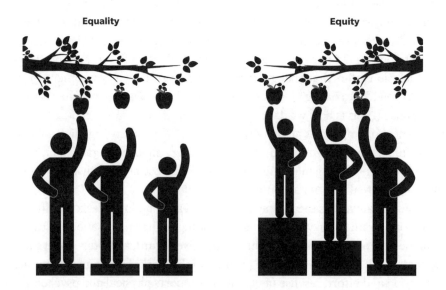

Equality   **Equity**

Wellness vs well-being

The words well-being and wellness tend to be used interchangeably in organisations, though they are really quite different, each having a distinct objective.

Well-being is about the individual experience of being within an organisation, considering how employees feel about their work, the climate and environment within which they work, the levels of stress they experience and their general happiness in the organisational context. Well-being largely focuses on engagement and performance as an objective. While, on the face of it, supporting well-being is something that should be commended, in reality, the efforts of organisations are largely exiguous and transactional, with employees rarely experiencing the benefits they are intended to deliver.

Wellness refers to programmes in organisations that support the physical and mental health of employees. Activities are designed to support healthier lifestyles, reduce the impact of the workplace on mental health and provide resources to improve diet and fitness. The objective is largely to reduce working days lost through illness and, in the USA, lower healthcare costs, saving money for the company. However, studies have shown that most programmes deliver little return on investment (ROI) and are, generally, not valued as much by employees as they are intended to. In fact, the flood of wellness programme providers to the market, who have little experience, research or qualification in providing their services and fail to take a holistic view of their approach, could be potentially damaging to some employees. For example, a *Harvard Business Review* article reported an employee, who was recovering from anorexia, sitting through a company workshop that promoted intermittent fasting as a path to healthy eating and lifestyle. The employee subsequently relapsed after berating herself for her lack of self-discipline, which was a fundamental aspect of the intermittent fasting process.

Community

A community is basically an organised social structure, which Charles H. Vogl describes in his book *The Art of Community* as being:

'A group of individuals who share a mutual concern for one another's welfare.'

A little simplistic perhaps as, if we look at the nature of communities, there are five broad categories, depending on the purpose that brought them together:

1 *Interest:* shared interest or passion.

2 *Action:* people trying to bring about change.

3 *Place:* a physical, geographical community.

4 *Practice:* people in the same profession or who undertake the same activities.

5 *Circumstance:* people brought together by events/situations.

None of these descriptions will guarantee that members will share concern for one another's welfare and, indeed, some indicate that there is more of an association within the community. For example, people in the same profession may consider themselves a part of a professional network, but the primary concern is the profession as an entity itself. However, the essence of community, which applies within organisations, where there is a strong sense of belonging, is that it is the needs of all members that come first.

Intersectionality

Intersectionality describes the range of characteristics an individual has, such as race, gender, disability, socio-economic status or religion, for example, which overlap and intersect, creating unique types of discrimination and privilege. Studies have been able to demonstrate hierarchy of disadvantage, where overlapping characteristics can create significant oppression. One study identified non-white disabled women as the most disadvantaged, outlining the grievous oppression and economic insecurity they suffer. This means that the traditional D&I approach of focusing on distinct categories of marginalisation is becoming less and less relevant. Focusing on belonging means focusing on the individuals as being distinct and creating an environment that supports all identities.

Neurodiversity

Neurodiversity describes the natural range of differences in human brain function, including autism, dyspraxia, dyslexia and attention deficit hyperactivity disorder (ADHD). Considering these differences as *natural* variations in the human genome is in contrast to most research over the past century (which treated variations as disorders or illnesses). As a result, until recently, there has, generally, been a poor understanding of people who are neurodivergent and, as a consequence, their opportunities and potential have been limited. This has come at a cost to organisations and societies, as well as to those individuals affected.

The term neurodiversity was first coined by Judy Singer, and described in her book *NeuroDiversity: The Birth of an Idea*. Here, Singer explored the need for a 'Neurodiversity Movement' and a greater understanding of autism and identity (following her own diagnosis and that of her daughter). Singer writes from a 'social constructionist view of disability', which means understanding disability in terms of how society is organised, rather than by an individual's impairment or difference. By thinking about neurodiversity in this way, and particularly within the workplace, we can see how standard practices may prevent individuals from using their talents to the best of their ability.

Given that between 10–15 per cent of the UK population is neurodivergent in some way, it is vital that organisations quickly understand how they can accommodate the challenges and tap into the unique talents of this population. Neurodivergent conditions are protected by legislation in many countries but the true advantage of understanding and supporting this population lies in the potential for innovation driven by their different thinking styles and perspectives.

Hidden differences

Hidden differences are things that people choose to disclose or hide. The term 'coming out' has long been recognised as a term referring to the LGBTQ+ communities, but many do not recognise that this term is also used in communities of people with hidden disabilities, such as neurodivergent employees or those with chronic illness. In doing so, they would be able to ask for the required reasonable adjustments and explain the specific challenges they face so that they could perform at their best, rather than being thought of as 'weird' or 'lazy', for example. But disclosure means they could face being stigmatised and seen as lacking, with both performance and careers suffering as a result. By not disclosing, they are forced to 'mask' – a word used particularly in the autistic community – which can be exhausting and, over a sustained period of time, can lead to burnout and mental health issues.

Mental health awareness has improved dramatically over the past few years, but there is still stigma related to mental illness, which means that employees who suffer feel uncomfortable in disclosing their conditions. This may be out of shame or fear of it impacting their job security, potential for career progression or their relationships with colleagues. The same also applies to some employees who suffer with other hidden chronic illnesses. While it is a personal choice to not disclose, there are some organisational cultures that exacerbate the problem – for example, those where any weakness is seen as a failing, where taking time off sick is frowned upon or where toxic, highly political cultures mean employees are apt to exploit the weaknesses of colleagues for their own gain.

Whatever the reason, keeping a part of identity or suffering hidden indefinitely isn't good for mental health under any circumstances and organisations have a moral responsibility to ensure they nurture a culture where psychological safety is protected at all costs to prevent any unnecessary suffering.

Code-switching and stereotype threat

The word 'code-switching' originally referred to moving between different languages, depending on the context. Today, it has been adopted by marginalised groups, particularly in the workplace, who feel that they have to deny parts of their own identity and adopt language, attitudes and activities associated with the dominant profile in the organisation. Sometimes, these will be visible differences, but the individual feels that, in order to fit in, they must mimic the majority – black employees have talked about 'speaking like a white person' or 'whitening' their CVs to ensure they can maximise their chances of being called to interview. Women may find that they must accept and join in with 'banter' or match the aggressive behaviour of men in meetings. They are fed reams of information about how to conduct themselves, how to be assertive and how to write emails without appearing deferential. Women are constantly being fed messages on how not to be female.

Stereotype threat describes the fear women and minority group employees may have about inadvertently confirming negative stereotypes regarding their group. It has been proven to have a significant effect on performance and advancement, and initiatives to drive inclusion, such as diversity training, often exacerbate stereotype threat, creating greater marginalisation.

These additional pressures on employees in the workplace can, as with autistic 'masking', lead to stress, anxiety and other mental health issues. It is behaviours such as these that highlight the critical link between a sense of belonging within an organisation and well-being.

part 1

The need for belonging

chapter 1

Why belonging is key to D&I initiatives

Progress on D&I in organisations has been underwhelming and patchy, despite the well-intended efforts, knowledge and passion of those within the profession. So, where is it going wrong?

In this chapter, I will look at why traditional D&I programmes haven't worked and why belonging must be where organisations focus their efforts for inclusion both now and in the future. The chapter will:

- help you to understand the psychological need to belong, which we all share, and the consequences of feeling that we do not belong

- explain why belonging is a critical need in an increasingly divided, uncertain world, where the nature of identity and the future of work are evolving at pace

- outline why D&I in organisations isn't working and how the current measures don't give a complete picture of how D&I is experienced by employees

- provide guidance on how to gather data to better understand the employee experience

Why D&I in organisations isn't working

An increasingly divided world

As the saying goes, we live in extraordinary times. But I am not sure a phrase exists that could do justice to the almost dystopian events of recent history and the world in which we are living today. We are seeing an increasing polarisation of opinion in so many aspects of life. The digital world is becoming ever more sophisticated at feeding us tailored information. This creates echo chambers of like-minded people, validating opinions, however extreme, and confirming belonging within the 'in-group' – whichever group that may be. According to Ofcom's Adults' Media Use and Attitudes Report,[1] in 2017, 18 per cent of people surveyed said that they rarely heard any news or media comment that they didn't agree with. By 2018, this was up to 25 per cent.[2] Our opinions are confirmed over and over again to the point where we come to believe them as fact – and, therefore, increasingly polarise 'us' and 'them'.

The rhetoric in US and UK politics is becoming increasingly divisive. There is no middle of the road. Increasingly polarised opinions are demonstrated at their worst by hate crime figures in both the UK and the USA. In July 2016, following the EU Referendum, the number of reported religiously and racially motivated hate crimes in the UK spiked and was 44 per cent higher than in July 2015. In November 2018, the FBI reported that US hate crimes had risen for the third consecutive year since Donald Trump's election – something that has been dubbed the 'Trump Effect' by US media. We could probably take an educated guess that the reported figures do not reflect the true extent of these crimes, as many go unreported, with victims being reluctant to come forward for fear of reprisal.

In May 2020, tension regarding ever-widening social inequalities, highlighted by the global pandemic, reached break point when the world shook as George Floyd, a 46-year-old black man from Minneapolis, USA, was killed at the hands of a white police officer. Recorded by witnesses, the video of the scene was pretty soon making its way around the world. Protests spread across the USA and then the world. In the UK, demonstrators started demanding the removal of historical statues that had links to white supremacy and the slave trade. Counter protests arose, with far-right protestors taking to the streets sparking violent conflicts with the police. (The irony, which is indicative of the increasing complexity of 'in' and 'out' groups today, was seen in action as many of the protestors used Nazi salutes during their march to save the statues of Winston Churchill, the man who had led the British defeat against the Nazis . . .)

In turn, we have seen increasing polarity in politics. On the one hand, there are those who believe we should dismantle systemic racism, that is the inequities about race based on history, institutions and culture. On the other, a backlash, are those fighting back with calls for meritocracy and nationalism. While these opposing ideologies are not new, the accusations hurled from each side of the argument are becoming more and more extreme with labels of communism and fascism. These divides signal a looming culture war that could have a significant impact on organisations.

In addition, we are increasingly seeing a polarisation between men and women. The #Metoo campaign – a step forward for women – is being countered by the angry rise of male supremacists. Anders Breivik, who murdered 77 people in Norway in 2011, was candid about the fact that he was partially motivated by a hatred of feminists, who he deemed poison and a threat to male-dominated society. Likewise, Elliot Rodger, who killed six people in California, in 2014, was motivated by a desire to punish women for rejecting him. A community self-named Incels (involuntary celibates) are becoming increasingly prevalent online, with a vitriolic narrative that encourages hatred and violence towards women. The rise in male supremacy groups is another worrying escalation of this ideology. Return of Kings and A Voice for Men are two such groups, who openly advocate physical and sexual violence towards women. Both organisations don't exist just online, where views can remain anonymous and vitriol can be spouted by way of a keyboard. There are conferences, meet-ups and even branded merchandise. Members and followers are publicly proud to be a part of these groups.

Our need to belong to a collective creates what are termed 'in-groups' and 'out-groups' – effectively, 'us' and 'them'. To reinforce our position in these collectives, we have a desire to make the out-group look bad, to boost the standing of our 'in-group'. But, in such extreme environments, the widening gulf between the two creates even more intense resentment and has far-reaching consequences.

It is quite easy to sit and read these stories, shaking our heads in horror and disbelief, safe in the knowledge that this is happening somewhere else, by and between others, that we are no part of it and have no responsibility for it. But let's think about these violations as a continuum. On the one extreme, there are violent, aggressive extremist behaviours. On the other, microaggressions – small, seemingly innocuous, behaviours or actions that communicate hostility or rejection. Aggressions, though small, serve the same purpose of signalling that somebody does not belong. Can we all, hand on heart, honestly say that we have not been guilty of this on occasion?

The impact of the divisive rhetoric in society will, inevitably, have an impact on workplace behaviours. With extremity of polarisation, overt or covert aggression is more likely. Political extremes and media echo chambers mean that people are more likely to be vocal in their opinions, bringing societal culture wars into the workplace.

Now, more than ever, organisations have a responsibility to ensure that they create an environment where aggressions of any kind are not tolerated and the well-being of all their employees is safeguarded. The focus has to shift from the tired paradigm of D&I, a term which in itself implies 'us and them', to creating a culture of belonging. A paradigm that protects all individuals from emotional and physical harm, drives productivity and innovation, deflects the risks posed by the current polarisation of society and values the unique identity of every employee.

The evolving nature of identity

Change in the world is rocketing in every sense and some changes are more or less comfortable depending on who you are. Within the workplace, indeed society as a whole, the nature of identity is becoming increasingly diverse and individual. With each new generation that enters the workplace, we will see more and more acceptance of individuality, and there is increasing pressure on organisations to adapt to this reality.

It is estimated that at some point between 2041 and 2046, minorities will be the majority in the USA, demographics that are reflected worldwide. The generation entering the workforce now have very different views on identity from those leaving it. This could, potentially, leave organisations at an impasse, given the often-polarised views of these different generations. However, with the future looking so different in terms of diversity, the approaches used today will be largely irrelevant.

Studies have been able to demonstrate the hierarchy of disadvantage, where overlapping characteristics can create significant oppression. A 2018 study published in *Gender and Society* identified non-white disabled women as the most disadvantaged, outlining the grievous oppression and economic insecurity they suffer. For this to stop, three things must happen:

1 The organisation should acknowledge that they do not understand the unique experiences of discrimination people face and open up the difficult conversations.

2 The organisation should be open about and acknowledge where there is both discrimination and privilege. Until we start talking about the unfair

advantage that some people have, rather than just the disadvantages of others, the power will remain with the privileged.

3 There needs to be a shift in focus from inclusion of certain groups to belonging for everyone. Categorising in this way hasn't worked so far, so certainly won't work in the future. If your organisation celebrates the increase in women in the organisation, but fails to acknowledge that, apart from binary gender, the increase has not increased the diversity of ethnicity, education background or anything else, then your efforts have done nothing but make a subtle statement about privilege.

Millennials and Generation Z (Gen Z), who now make up the majority of the global workforce, increasingly see identity as being multi-dimensional. Globalisation and migration mean that ethnicity and race are no longer as simple as a few tick boxes. The upcoming generations question the importance of authorities anywhere wanting to categorise them according to their gender at birth. Gender is no longer seen as binary, and is considered multi-faceted. Language around gender is changing significantly and many people in organisations who are not familiar with it may be dismissive because they lack understanding. Since 2016, people in New York City have been able to choose from a minimum of 31 gender identities – a standard that has been brought in by the city's Commission on Human Rights. Any business that ignores the standard, and does not accommodate all identities, faces a hefty fine.

Intersectionality means that, in the future, categorising diversity as we do now will be impossible and, potentially, illegal. There is no way of telling how quickly these identities or the law will evolve, but this certainly means that D&I initiatives as they are today will be obsolete. Optimistically, we could hope that this could signal the end of discrimination in the workplace, but stereotyping, bias and collective identity are constructs that are core to human psychology. However, at this stage, we have no idea what collectives may evolve or which groups could potentially be marginalised. Therefore, in preparing organisational cultures for this future, we need to start focusing on creating a culture of belonging now.

Identity as a determinant of privilege and disadvantage

To date, D&I in organisations has focused largely on visible, ascriptive (inherent attributes) groups, but, recently, the narrative has started to change, considering the privilege or disadvantage that acquired differences can engender (Figure 1.1). The list of characteristics below is by no means exhaustive, but demonstrates the scope for overlapping characteristics to increase or decrease advantage.

Figure 1.1 The intersectionality model showing those who are most likely to be privileged or disadvantaged

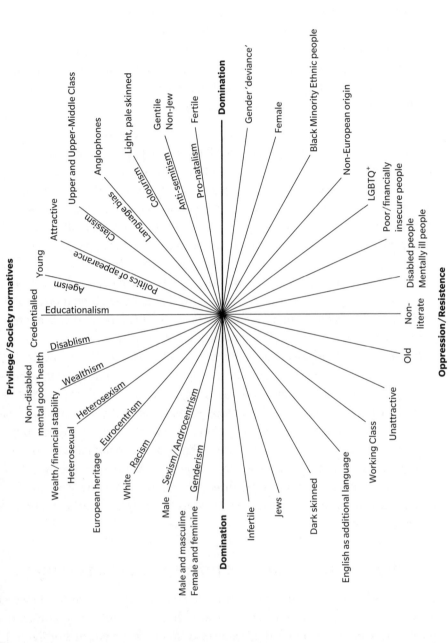

Race	This refers to biology and physical characteristics, such as skin and hair colour. The narrative around exclusion on this basis has been around for a long time, yet progress has been slow. Sadly, racial discrimination as a priority in organisations mostly relies on corporate lawyers advising boards to mitigate risk, after widely reported cases such as the George Floyd murder bring the issue into the spotlight.
Ethnicity	Different from race, ethnicity describes shared language, culture or history in a group within which individuals identify, such as Jewish, Hispanic or Kurdish people, often with a shared history of persecution. However, little is discussed about the fact that White British and White American are also ethnic groups, who have a history of privilege – which largely remains in the workplaces of today.
Gender	Cisgender (gender assigned at birth) men generally remain the most advantaged gender in the workplace, but, as there is a move away from binary gender, discrimination against those who do not fit into these two categories is becoming more prevalent. In one piece of research, an architect describes how clients stopped hiring her after she transitioned and reported many examples of employees whose colleagues passive-aggressively demonstrate their objections by refusing to use preferred pronouns (referring to him, her or they, with some people preferring to use gender-neutral or gender-inclusive pronouns, which do not associate a gender with the individual).
Sexual orientation/ identity	Sexual diversity and identity have changed exponentially within the course of one generation. Millennials and Gen Z largely accept the diverse and dynamic nature of sexuality, but there is still a lack of willingness to recognise these different identities, particularly in older generations.
Ability	Physical disability in organisations tends to be treated as an accessibility issue rather than as a marginalised ascriptive group, like gender or race. In addition, those with hidden differences, such as chronic illness, mental health issues or neurodivergent conditions, can face inadvertent discrimination due to a lack of understanding from managers and colleagues.
Physical qualities	This group includes any ascriptive qualities that somebody may have, for example birth defects or height. These work to create disadvantage and privilege, with many studies demonstrating the advantage tall or attractive employees have in terms of career prospects.
Religion	Religion, usually accompanied by a particular race or ethnicity, can lead to significant discrimination. Religious symbols, such as the hijab, can become an object of mockery or scorn, and discrimination often increases in relation to external events, such as 9/11.

Socio-economic background	Socio-economic background can lead to considerable privilege or disadvantage, remarkably so in some industries. Those from lower socio-economic backgrounds are significantly under-represented in senior roles and may face regular, subtle discrimination through mocking of accents or so-called 'banter'. Studies show that those perceived to have lower socio-economic status are significantly more likely than others to face bullying in the workplace.
Parental/ carer status	Parental status carries more than just the juggle of work and parenting. It includes disadvantage suffered by those who may have frequent miscarriages, are going through IVF or have to care for children with chronic illnesses. It may be the slurs that are aimed at women who have children in quick succession. Carer status brings with it the same juggle as parenting, though less predictable and often with very little support.
Education	This includes both the level of education achieved, the type of schooling and the status of institutions. There is often a perception that, because somebody has a specific education, they are more intelligent, competent or worthy than someone else. This affects hiring decisions, career advancement and the level of respect people receive in the workplace.

Who are you?

The first step in your journey towards leadership that focuses on belonging is to work on your own acceptance of all identities.

First, consider the table of characteristics above and build a picture of your identity profile. Write a description of yourself against each of the characteristics.

Now, go through the list again and, being completely honest with yourself, think about where some of your biases may lie or which identities you find it difficult to relate to and/or accept. Consider why you feel that way and what you gain from holding that view. Is it driven by lack of understanding or fear? Does it protect the status of your identity?

Look at the last 10 people you texted on your phone:

- How different is their profile from yours?

Now, think about some of the people on your team:

- How different are their profiles from yours?
- Do you think that you have a rounded view of each of these identities?
- Do you recognise any biases you consciously or subconsciously have regarding any of these identities?

Take some time to think about this and what this means for you as a leader:

- Where do you have the strongest relationships in your team?
- Are they more like you and do you know more about them than others?
- In your network, do you gravitate more towards people who are like you or do you seek out people who are different?

Now, consider what you might be able to do to increase the diversity of people you interact with, such as:

- Spending time getting to know more about the people in your team or peers who are very different from you.
- When you need advice, rather than your usual 'go-to' people, consider seeking out the perspective of someone who is very different from you.
- Ask for more opinions and advice from more junior team members.
- Regularly ask for feedback from people who are different from you.
- Consider getting involved in different employee networks to gain understanding about different groups.

The future of work

The history of the office as the 'workplace' can be traced back to the East India Company in London in the 17th century. Without technology, the need to provide a space that centralised communication, monitored performance and created structure for workers was critical for an organisation that was trading globally. Accounts from workers at the time demonstrate the importance of identity and social connectivity within a defined 'workplace', as well as the risk of well-being issues in a restrictive regime and confined space (there are many accounts of employees committing suicide by throwing themselves from the windows of the building).

Fast forward 400 years. Technology in the late 20th century advanced at an unprecedented scale and continues exponentially in the changing world of the 21st. The idea of 'telecommuting' is over 50 years old and, yet, despite an increasing need to connect with employees and clients globally, as well as an increase in connective technologies, this way of working 'virtually' has been slow to evolve. The office, despite the construct being designed for a pre-technology world, is the mainstay for all but a very small proportion of organisations.

But the generations who occupy the workplace are changing. They are more used to the virtual world than their predecessors. The World Economic Forum's annual convention in Davos in January 2020, regarding the future of work, reported that, for the first time, Generation Z (those born between 1997 and 2012) and Millennials (those born between 1981 and 1996) make up the majority of the workforce worldwide. Their emphatic conclusions about the future of work and talent were reported as:

> **'Younger workers are looking for more decentralised environments where they can decide how work gets done.'**

And:

> **'Specifically, everyone must ask themselves . . . how do we disrupt our outdated ways of doing things? How do we challenge ourselves to deviate from conventional business practice? Only that way will we be prepared for unpredictability in the job market.'**

Fast forward again – this time, just six weeks. As the World Health Authority announced a global COVID-19 pandemic, and subsequent lockdowns ensued, businesses across the world were forced to make changes. Teams had to swiftly adapt their working practices on an unprecedented scale. New skills had to be developed as video-conferencing replaced office meeting rooms, businesses had to find new ways to connect with customers and clients and leaders found themselves with the difficult tasks of protecting the emotional welfare of their employees while implementing management practice that would ensure there was as little business interruption as feasibly possible.

As lockdown continued, businesses started to re-invent, innovate, find their flow, try new things and adapt to the limitations of a global pandemic. Automation, innovation and digitisation increased faster and on a scale never seen before. We were living in our predicted future. As the pandemic advanced and peaked, the unpredictability of what the near future held, and lessons learned from the changing nature of work, caused many to start making predictions about the 'new normal', acknowledging that things are very unlikely to go back to the way they were before.

This event highlighted one certainty. Volatility is, almost certainly, set to be a hallmark of the future of work. This is not the last crisis (or indeed pandemic) we will face in our lifetimes. Virtual connectivity will become a permanent feature of at least some team interactions and the challenge for organisations is this – how do we create inclusion, belonging and protection of the well-being of employees in this brave new world?

Where is D&I going wrong?

In the 2020 Deloitte 'Global Human Capital Trends' survey, belonging and well-being topped the list as the two most reported human capital priorities for organisations. The report stated:

'79% of organisations agreed "fostering a sense of belonging in the workforce is important or very important for their success over the next 12 to eighteen months".
'Yet only 13% said there were plans in place and were ready to do so.'

This shift was initially slow to gain momentum, but was expedited by the uncertainty and changing nature of the workplace in 2020. In an increasingly virtual world, leaders looked for ways to preserve their cultures, to maintain a sense of connectivity both within teams and to the organisation, and to protect the well-being of employees to support business continuity in such unprecedented times.

In addition, it was reported by McKinsey that the crisis had advanced organisations 10 years in 90 days in terms of innovation and digital transformation. Organisations had to face the reality that sustained speed of transformation and innovation are set to define the 'new normal'. The ability of organisations to implement ways of working to embed, drive and sustain this will be a critical determinant of future performance.

With this in mind, let's look first at why current D&I practice is failing to meet these cultural, well-being and performance priorities.

The truth behind the headlines: D&I is not a priority in most organisations

'Diverse and inclusive cultures are providing companies with a competitive edge over their peers.'

We are used to seeing these headlines and being bombarded by the stats published by organisations to demonstrate their success in leveraging performance through D&I. If this is the case, then, surely, we don't need to change what we are doing? It is working, so let's leave it as it is and put belonging back in its box, right?

You see, I have a problem with these headlines. I am in no way suggesting they are untrue – these organisations probably do have a range of D&I initiatives going on, have made progress on quotas and may, indeed, have seen an increase in performance. The problem is that, in the majority of cases, this is more likely to be correlation and *not* causation. The old adage 'money is a dirty word' comes to mind when we dig deeper into the mercenary truth that often lies beneath the success headlines.

So, let's get it out there: the nature of organisations means that D&I simply isn't a priority. Organisational priorities are informed by financial targets and risk mitigation (which, in reality, mean the same thing – money). Until we are willing to talk about and address this, then plans are doomed to fail from the start. The model in Figure 1.2 demonstrates why this is the case.

Most organisations only take action and prioritise an issue when it has financial and legal implications, and this is where the root of the challenge lies. If I feel that I don't belong and I am being treated unfairly by somebody who is impeding belonging, then I am significantly less likely to make a complaint than someone who feels that they do belong. The situation would, therefore, impact both my performance and well-being – both of which impair my ability to be able to deliver results. My behaviours are then questioned as the potential source of my performance issues.

However, the individual who feels that they do belong and is treating me unfairly does deliver results, so there is no incentive for the behaviour to be addressed – even if other people are very aware of the poor behaviour. So, the cycle continues and the belonging issues remain. Despite the mounting evidence that, in the long term, performance of diverse organisations is significantly increased, this just isn't enough to risk short-term gains.

Figure 1.2 The difficult truth about why D&I initiatives fail

An example

The headline:

'On average diverse organisations had a profit margin of 8% higher than those at the bottom of the rankings, with the financial services industry leading the way'

The truth:

A firm is publicly committed to increasing the number of female leaders, and invests a lot of time and effort into a programme to do so. This includes giving all leaders targets, related to bonus pay outs, regarding recruitment, retention and promotion of female leaders. Sounds good, right? However, in relation to the bonus percentage based on financial targets, this is relatively low. In one team, the highest revenue generator frequently demonstrates overtly aggressive behaviours particularly directed towards a female colleague. He often does this publicly and the manager of the team is well aware of the situation. The female colleague speaks to the manager about how this is impacting her and he addresses it with the male colleague several times, but the situation continues. It gets to the point where the female colleague is finding it intolerable and is considering leaving the organisation. If you were the line manager, what would you (honestly) do? If the female colleague leaves, you will miss out on a small part of your bonus. But, if the male leaves, the impact on financial targets will be catastrophic and you are well aware of the potential damage to your career. It is a classic 'Catch 22', firmly underpinned by organisational culture.

This is a situation I see and hear about regularly. The potential impact of diversity on the bottom line is not factored into leaders' diversity targets and, therefore, not realised. Toxic behaviours are left unchecked and kept away from the top of the organisation by managers. Financial performance looks healthy and organisations are keen to publicise the link between profits and increased diversity. Meanwhile, within the organisation, marginalised employees are 'strongly advised' not to make a formal complaint. HR ward off the risk by warning them that an investigation would be extensive, involving many people and could, potentially, be damaging to the employee's professional reputation, as well as their relationships with colleagues. These situations are often treated as an individual rather than cultural problem.

Those that do take their cases further, are pressured into settling out of court and signing an NDA. Research by *Financial News* of the UK financial services industry indicated that approximately 80 per cent of sex discrimination cases are 'withdrawn', 17 per cent are lost and just 3 per cent are won. Even those that win find the process to be so traumatic and damaging to their careers that they advise others against doing the same. Information on other marginalised groups in this context appears to be non-existent. These stats give an indication of what is really going on but never make the headlines like the increased performance and diversity success. The reputations of the organisations involved remain intact.

So, the reality of the actual experience of employees remains hidden. Most organisations are not incentivised to dig deep and ask the difficult questions because the status quo presents very little risk. Nobody wants to open Pandora's box because, once they do, they know they will have to act. Most of the initiatives implemented by organisations are highly visible and can be easily measured, such as minority representation, external PR initiatives or transactional training programmes.

This simply is not good enough. In a 2019 global survey, 'Workplace Diversity, Inclusion, and Intersectionality', 80 per cent of straight white men agreed that people from all backgrounds have equal opportunities to succeed in their organisation, compared to only 54 per cent of black women and 58 per cent of LGBTQ+ women.[3] I could say that the situation isn't improving, but, in fact, it could be getting worse as we start to see the rise of 'modern racism' – the belief that racial and other minorities are no longer discriminated against and receive undeserved special treatment. The difficult questions are not being asked, resources are being wasted on programmes and initiatives that do not work. So, what else should we be asking? What is it that we cannot see? And what is it that we are ignoring?

See no evil, speak no evil, hear no evil

As outlined above, much of the exclusion within organisations goes ignored, is covered up or else is unreported. Severance agreements silence those who may have been victims, people stay quiet because they don't want to be labelled a troublemaker and witnesses turn a blind eye because it is not their problem. Organisations suffer from what we could call the 'Harvey Weinstein effect' – discriminative behaviour often happens at very senior levels and people know that calling it out would be career suicide.

Diverse representation becomes narrower the further up the ladder you go – and this is not necessarily because of lack of opportunity. The majority of decision makers in organisations are white men over 45. Recent research also shows that maternity and motherhood cannot be attributed entirely to women's lack of progress. As a coach, I have spoken to many women who get to a certain level in the organisation and then self-select out. Why? Because the general approach to inclusion in organisations is to give people the opportunity to progress with the unspoken proviso that they must then 'include' themselves. Female senior leaders are often lonely in their positions and find the culture in the leadership teams intolerable. They may feel unheard and insignificant. And, so, the group-think associated with the homogeny of leadership teams continues. Alongside this, the feeling of not belonging leads to those with hidden differences masking their challenges, minorities code-switching and all those who feel marginalised working under the shadow of stereotype threat.

We talk about bottom-up and top-down initiatives, ignoring the fact that the critical challenge may be the middle. Engagement and culture surveys don't ask the really difficult questions, the ones that would expose where toxicity lies, and give a view of what is really happening on the ground. Surveys ask:

'Do you feel valued at work?'

Rather than:

'In the past 12 months, has anyone in the organisation made you feel that you are worthless or unimportant? If so, how often have you felt this way? Please provide further detail.'

which would give significantly greater insight into what the issues are and where the problems lie. We keep the idea of inclusion to distinct, easily meas-ured categories, ignoring the fact that there are a lot more reasons why people feel excluded that don't necessarily fit into a neat category. In one report, more than half of all the respondents who could fit into the diversity bracket said they saw bias as a typical part of their day-to-day experience at work. On the other hand, white heterosexual males, who are the most prominent leadership profile in the study, think that decision making is free from bias and that bias was not experienced on a day-to-day basis in diverse groups.[4]

Most initiatives are failing because they are, at best, transactional and smack of tokenism.

The lion's den

Many D&I plans lead with recruitment and representation, often with little or no effort to change the culture across the organisation, or to provide education that supports belonging. For example, there are organisations that embrace D&I but fail to consider what needs to happen in the wider organisation to ensure that the understanding of some minority groups will create a sense of belonging.

Take, for example, a 2019 tribunal awarded against npower, who was committed to D&I and was publicly explicit about this. When an employee was diagnosed with autism and an associated anxiety disorder, his line manager failed to make the recommended reasonable adjustments to his working environment, which were significantly contributing to his anxiety. In addition, his manager did not equate this anxiety with his performance, which was suffering immeasurably. His employment was subsequently terminated after a lengthy and stressful capability process. It was an unfortunate situation for all involved and highlights how critical education is for ensuring everyone is treated with respect. A little understanding can go a long way.

A coaching client told me once that it is common practice in meetings across her organisation for men to talk or shout over women and take out their phones when a woman is presenting. It was commonly discussed among women in the organisation but, when she suggested to her line manager that she would like to 'call it out' next time she witnessed this, she was 'strongly advised against doing so'. Such statements are strong cultural markers, indicating 'this is how we do things round here'.

In my work, I have come across countless situations like this. Organisations that are able to demonstrate, through data, that they have diverse teams and that they have, for example, higher than average female promotion to senior leadership. There is no reason at all to doubt the integrity of the CEOs and executive boards, but, inside, the organisation often tells a very different story. Statistics say very little about the actual experience of employees:

- There is little appetite to embrace inclusive leadership and, therefore, deal with behaviours detrimental to belonging.

- Minorities are advised against standing up to these behaviours, sometimes being given exponential pay increases to keep them happy while being sidelined into bland projects where they can't cause any issues for the leader.

- Those who raise grievances are often seen as 'troublemakers' who are often paid off if they persist with and escalate their complaints.

- Mental health issues are closely related to feeling excluded or discriminated against. However, these employees will mask their suffering to prevent them from looking any weaker, as signs of emotion in organisations are often met with a roll of the eyes.

And, I am going to say it: the 'B' word that seldom features in the D&I narrative and one of the most taboo in corporate language; the word that strikes the fear of God into HR directors. Bullying. The behaviours, often subtle and appearing innocuous (though sometimes loud and overtly aggressive in toxic cultures), that create significant suffering for some, yet are largely ignored by everyone else. Why does it become less important when it is not on the grounds of a legally protected status, such as gender or race? The answer is in the question – it is not a priority because it carries less risk from a legal and reputation perspective.

If this is happening in your organisation, flip the narrative. Instead of allowing one person to feel shame every day at the hands of someone else, bring shame upon the perpetrators. Show the rest of the organisation that this is not acceptable on any level. Policies and words do not equate to action and will never bring about lasting change. Put the moral responsibility on organisations to protect their employees from *any* harm right up there as a priority with results and risk. Do the right thing. In the long term, it will pay.

These are the unpalatable truths that very few companies are acknowledging. The unspoken reality that is not published in reports by management consultancies. There are many companies who report great D&I progress and proudly relate this to how they are outperforming competitors. Dig deeper, ask employees about their experience and often you will find it is through more mercenary activities that the company is succeeding. Paying equal pay, fast-tracking promotion and targeting leaders on inclusive leadership without addressing the real issues is just smoke and mirrors. Not equating bullying behaviour with exclusion and failing to address toxic behaviours at all levels will not create a belonging culture. Paying off 'trouble-makers' who raise grievances will not create a belonging culture. These actions are consolidating existing cultures and jeopardising the well-being of employees.

The 'work masks' employees wear and the impact on well-being

In the definition of belonging at work, I referred to individual, subjective experience of belonging and connectedness. This places identity as central to belonging and, therefore, being accepted for who you are is critical to connectedness. Current D&I practice has had very little impact on those who feel the need to hide aspects of their identity in order to be accepted. Maintaining any pseudo-identity for a sustained period of time can lead to stress, anxiety and disengagement. Organisations and leadership texts talk of 'bringing your authentic self to work'. In an unsupportive environment, this can be difficult for anyone – but for those who feel the need to adapt their identity, it can have a significant impact on mental health, which leads to a further dimension of exclusion.

There are many subtle cues in organisations that underpin this need to adapt identity. Take, for example, dress codes – not uniforms or clothing required for safety, but standards outlined in policy where these are not required. Unsurprisingly, the narrative and debate around dress code centres largely around what can be stated without being discriminatory with regards to legislation. For example, policy should not discriminate between genders, as per a recent case in the UK where a female temporary employee was sent home for not wearing high heels. However, until now, this debate has focused largely on the nature of sex and gender being binary, but there is emerging recognition of the complexity of dress code given increasing acceptance of the non-binary nature of sex and gender. This means dress code policies could, potentially, discriminate against the legally protected statuses of sexual orientation and transgender.

Put simply, *no* person or organisation has the right to ask anybody to leave their identity at the door before they enter. Without acknowledging and addressing the above concerns, that is exactly what they are doing.

The absence of disability

When I read D&I reports and surveys by consulting firms, as well as commentary and literature elsewhere, I always notice there is one stark absence – disability. In the most recent annual D&I reports by McKinsey, Deloitte and Accenture, only Deloitte includes bias against disability as questions in its surveys; McKinsey mentions the word 'disabilities' only once in an example of a negative comment from the survey; and Accenture fails to mention it all.

A recent search of Google images for 'people diversity organisations' showed only two photographs in the first one hundred that include disabled people (actually, disabled person, as both of these appeared to be stock images which used the same female wheelchair user!). The narrative around diversity in organisations is largely excluding this group, not only preventing these employees from bringing their unique talents to the workplace, but also, almost certainly, impacting their well-being. Everyone included means everyone.

Belonging: the D&I refocus that will make all the difference

We all need to belong

'This sense of belonging that cannot be denied anyone, against which there are no arguments, can only be won by being involved, by cooperating, and experiencing, and by being useful to others. Out of this emerges a lasting, genuine feeling of worthiness.'

Alfred Adler, *Individual Psychology* (1926)

On the first day of school for both of my children, like many parents, I was an emotional wreck. Apart from this being the first step towards independence, as parents we worry that they may not fit in – that they might not feel a sense of belonging. What if no one will play with them? Will they sit and eat lunch alone? Stand on the playground waiting for someone to ask them to join in? Will they be sad or scared? Of course, the caricature of my children as social pariahs that I conjured up was completely out of proportion, but, because we all know how it feels when you feel like you don't belong, we can palpably feel it on behalf of others. Venturing out into the world alone for the first time, I knew that this could be the first time it was experienced by my children.

It was the psychoanalyst Alfred Adler (7 February 1870 – 28 May 1937), the father of 'Individual Psychology', who first identified this core need individuals have to belong and the relationship of this to our own self-esteem. It is a fundamental and powerful motivation, a hangover from our ancestral history when being part of a group was critical to our survival. We satisfy our need for belonging through bonds we make with family and friends, and search for groups to join to satisfy our desire for collective belonging. Our interpersonal lives are dominated by the need to be accepted by others and to avoid rejection, which then drives many of our behaviours. Recent research has suggested that human beings may be wired to feel pain when they are excluded or rejected from a group, just as evolution has wired us to feel pain when we are deprived of our basic needs such as food, water and shelter. Being accepted is critical to our sense of identity, our self-esteem and self-regulation, and being part of a group is affirmation of our social standing.

Given the power of this need and its similarity to other fundamental human needs, there are a raft of negative effects – both emotional and physical – which can result from perceived rejection or exclusion. These include:

- anxiety, stress and depression
- chronic mental health problems, if the situation is sustained over a period of time
- loneliness: researchers have shown that loneliness (which means a feeling of disconnectedness, not necessarily social isolation) can lead to a weakened immune system and, therefore, susceptibility to illness.

The desire to belong and be accepted is an essential part of being a human being, a need that must be met for the sake of mental and physical health and that, therefore, must be given consideration in the context of any organised collective. The powerful and fundamental need for belonging goes beyond inclusion and describes the experience a sense of belonging brings. The opportunities it presents and the potential risks it poses in its absence are too important for organisations to ignore.

Of all the collectives to which we belong, the workplace is the one where we will spend most of our time. On average, employees will spend approximately 90,000 hours in the workplace in their lifetime. Given that we spend almost a third of our lives in work, the impact of not feeling a sense of belonging there can have a significant impact on happiness, quality of life and well-being.

A Search for Belonging: the memoir of former Chief Constable Michael Fuller

Michael Fuller was born to Windrush-generation Jamaican immigrants in 1959 and, when he was 16, became a cadet in the Metropolitan Police. His career achievements here, and later in Kent as the first ever ethnic minority Chief Constable in the UK, were exceptional, including setting up the Racial and Violent Crime Task Force and the Operation Trident command unit, which successfully reduced gun crime in London.

In 2019, he published his memoir, which was originally called *Kill the Black One First*, and later changed to *A Search For Belonging: A Story About Race, Identity, Belonging and Displacement*. In the book, he recounts his personal journey growing up in care and his lifelong career in the police. Having been a childhood dream to join the police, he would never imagine that his career would be blighted by intentional and unintentional racism, and hatred from black communities who saw him as a traitor.

As the comments, 'banter' and unreasonable requests continued (such as being told by an inspector to 'Go and get some arrests and make sure one of them is black'), Michael chose to laugh along or obey commands because he knew it was the only way he could remain in the career he loved. In essence, in order to belong, he had to leave his identity at the door. Having introduced diversity training into the police, in an interview with the *Daily Express* newspaper in 2019, he lamented the fact that a black police officer had recently confided in him that he couldn't wait to leave the force because of the 'subtle racism' that still exists today.

During his time in Kent Police, reported crimes dropped by 22 per cent and Michael was awarded the Queen's Police Medal. However, despite this, in the 10 years since he retired, there has never been another black Chief Constable in the UK.

Michael's story is relevant to all teams, organisations and institutions. It demonstrates how the efforts of organisations are failing because they do not take into account the personal experiences of those who feel that they don't belong. The impact of this, demonstrated in this story, is that the efforts made internally by organisations, sufficient or not to advance the progress of minority groups, is thwarted by the personal experiences that make many talented individuals self-select out. This has implications for the challenges faced in both recruitment and retention, regarding the attraction and turnover of marginalised groups.

The perception gap

It is important to consider that the failure of D&I policy, exemplified in what has been covered so far, is not necessarily wilfully ignored or swept under the carpet by leaders. As we have seen, D&I metrics don't provide a view of the real experience of employees, so they may be forgiven for their apparent lack of action. The Accenture report 'Getting to Equal 2020' reported the following:

- Two-thirds of leaders feel they create empowering environments in which employees can be themselves, raise concerns and innovate without fear of failure, while just one-third of employees agree.

- More than three-quarters of leaders say employees have good control over when, where and how they work, while only 29 per cent of employees agree.

- 20 per cent of employees do not feel included in their organisations, feeling they are not welcome at work and can't contribute fully and thrive, while only 2 per cent of leaders feel the same.

This report highlights the problem of the perception gap – leaders falsely and unwittingly believing that there is a strong sense of belonging and empower-ment because this is what the D&I or engagement metrics reflect. More than that, where there is a perception gap regarding empowering environments, leaders should be seriously concerned about the cultural impact on employee engagement and well-being. Where people are afraid to raise concerns, leaders have no idea of how employees experience the organisation on a daily basis, pos-ing a risk to employee brand, well-being and performance.

The implicit values that differentiate belonging from traditional D&I are based on understanding experiences at an individual level and creating a cul-ture where the talent of all employees is enabled.

- The focus is on the individual human experience of belonging, not one size fits all.
- Belonging widens the scope of inclusion to everyone, not targeted groups.
- Belonging creates purpose at organisational, team and an individual level.
- Belonging marries social connectivity, performance and well-being – critical in an increasingly virtual world.
- Belonging reframes engagement to the more human perspective of connectiv-ity between the individual identity and the organisation.

A sense of belonging will ensure that diverse individuals and teams are able to collaborate in a way that drives performance through connectivity, agility and innovation, top priorities in today's climate.

When we work within diverse teams, where there is high engagement and strong psychological safety, we learn to respect a wide range of differing viewpoints, which can lead to better decision making and fostering of new ideas. Conversely, homogeneous teams, or those where some employees feel that they do not have a voice, are more prone to complacency and 'group-think', thereby unwittingly pro-moting stagnation and mediocrity. However, bringing together diverse thinking isn't easy. Innovation is an interactive process – communication and interaction within diverse teams needs to be facilitated to ensure all voices are heard, ideas are clearly communicated and a healthy level of conflict allows consensus to be reached. This is not an organic process, and diversity alone in an organisation will not in any way guarantee a sudden increase in innovation. The organisational structure, culture, leadership and behaviours must enable the right people, with the right talents to connect in a way that supports the sharing of diverse perspectives.

If organisations want to leverage performance and innovation through diversity, they simply must start creating a belonging culture.

Singapore – a belonging and performance success story

In the 2019 World Economic Forum article 'The business case for diversity in the workplace is now overwhelming', Vijay Eswaran, executive chairman of QI Group, cites the case of Singapore as an analogy for exemplar diversity practice. Singapore has a population of just over five million and, yet, today is recognised as one of the top financial centres in the world. The case for diversity is clearly evident in the multicultural population with a range of ethnicities and religions living and working peacefully alongside one another. However, to understand how they have managed to mobilise this diverse knowledge, we must look back to 1965 when Singapore first gained independence. From the start, the country's founders were intent on creating racial harmony and, to create the culture they wanted, they imposed strict policy measures such as communities in public housing complexes having national quotas of racial percentage. This foundation led to the harmony and success that Singapore still enjoys today. Leaders within organisations can learn from this – if you want to create a diverse and harmonious organisation that benefits from the innovation this can bring, the cause must be led aggressively from the top, and focus on actions that, in time, will develop a belonging culture.

Activity
Mind the perception gap!

Consider these perception gaps within the context of your organisation and current D&I initiatives.

The following are some common initiatives within D&I programmes. Using the table below, consider which of these you currently undertake, as well as adding any others you include, the measures you use to gauge success and whether these are sufficient to give you genuine understanding of the degree to which success is experienced on an individual level. This will give you an indication of which initiatives are genuinely giving you return on investment, as well as where 'perception gaps' may exist.

Examples

Initiative	KPI	Employee experience data
D&I targets	Female leader quotas	Women's networks Exit interviews Leadership development programmes
Recruitment training	Representation quotas	Candidate feedback
Inclusive HR policies and processes		
D&I targets		
Structured interview training		
Recruitment training		
Unconscious bias training		
Inclusive leadership programmes		
Cultural awareness training		
Inclusive recruitment training		
Gender diversity training		
Neurodiversity training		
Externally benchmarked D&I goals		
Inclusion training		
Race diversity training		
Managing diversity		
Strategic D&I training		
Dignity at work training		

Given the focus on data, here and in other parts of this book, it is critical to understand what you can and can't do. The majority of countries world-wide have data protection legislation in place – some have one compre-hensive legislation, such as GDPR in the EU, while others have a more complex series of laws, such as in the USA, where legislation may also differ slightly from state to state. Ensure you are aware of the data protec-tion legislation in place within your region and that any activity you carry out is compliant with this. Larger organisations will, almost certainly, have adapted HR data collection and retention practices in place, but, if you are unsure, or if you are just starting out, it would be wise to seek advice.

What percentage of your current programmes capture employee expe-rience data? Where you are lacking employee experience data, consider what data points you have access to that may help with further analysis.

Consider the entire employee lifecycle, which may include:

- demographic data
- recruitment data
- career progression data
- exit data
- absence data
- flexible working data
- engagement surveys
- inclusion surveys
- pulse surveys
- D&I focus groups
- employee networks
- performance data
- external D&I benchmarks
- salary data
- employee brand data
- grievance data.

Now list:

1 Which of these data points you have access to.
2 What employee experience data within the employee lifecycle you are missing.
3 Where in the employee lifecycle there are significant perception gaps.

This analysis is your starting point for building a business case for a belonging programme, which we will build upon in subsequent chapters.

Notes

---

1 https://www.ofcom.org.uk/__data/assets/pdf_file/0031/149872/Adults-media-use-and-attitudes-report-2019-chart-pack.pdf. Accessed on 26 May, 2021.

2 Saville Rossiter-Base Fieldwork: September to November 2018, based on 3,764 adults, aged 16+.

3 Culture Amp 2019 report, available at: https://www.cultureamp.com/2019-diversity-inclusion-report. Accessed on 26 May, 2021.

4 'Fixing the Flawed Approach to Diversity', 17 January 2019, Boston Consulting Group. 16,500 survey respondents. Available at: https://www.bcg.com/publications/2019/fixing-the-flawed-approach-to-diversity. Accessed on 26 May, 2021.

chapter 2

The Five Principles of Belonging

In this chapter, I will define the principles upon which a belonging culture can be built in organisations. Creating an environment where everyone feels a sense of belonging requires consideration of the whole organisation, not just a range of activities defined and implemented by a D&I team. It means consideration of processes, structures, leadership, team principles and individual identities. With this in mind, this chapter will include:

- how redefining organisations from a 'community' perspective can support the development of a belonging culture
- how a sense of purpose can be embedded through the principles of belonging
- the key cultural attributes that create belonging and the role of individual employees, leadership and teams within this context
- guidance on how to start a high-level assessment of your organisation against the characteristics of an organisation-community

Figure 2.1 The Five Principles of Belonging

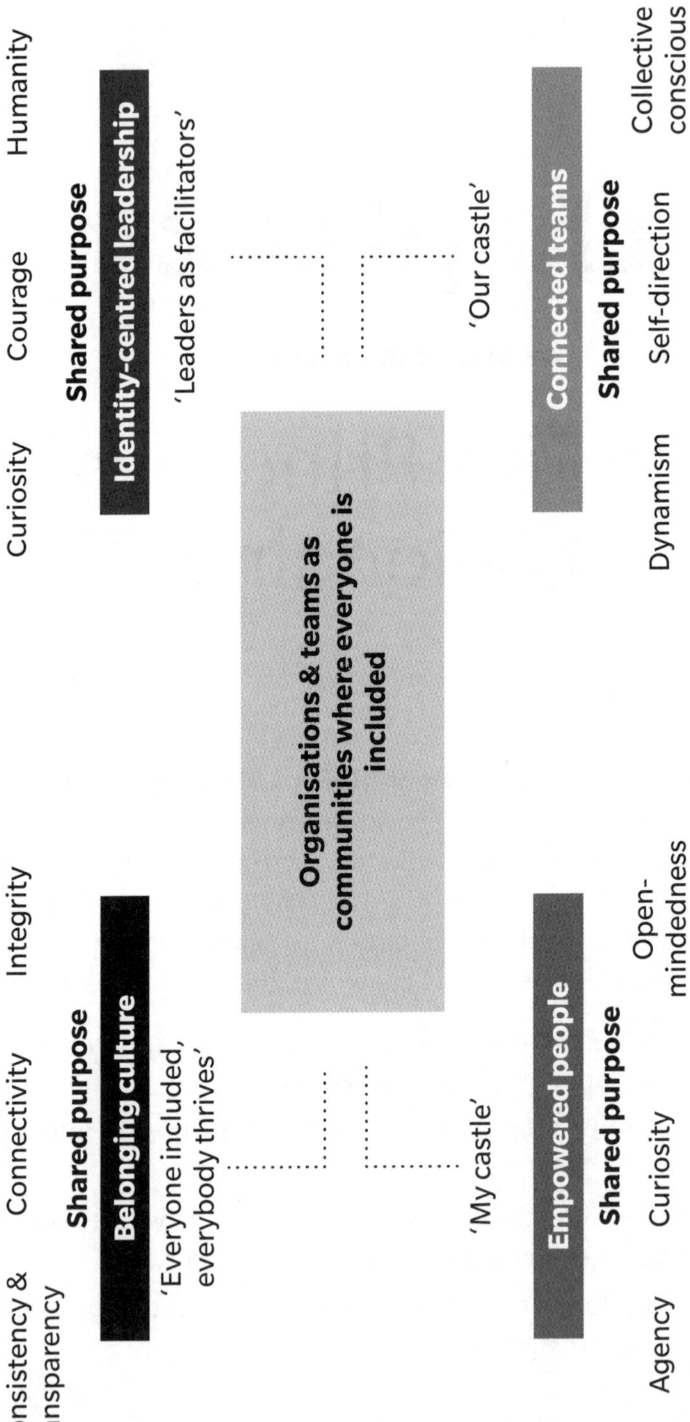
Consistency & transparency
Connectivity
Integrity
Shared purpose
Belonging culture
'Everyone included, everybody thrives'
Curiosity
Courage
Humanity
Shared purpose
Identity-centred leadership
'Leaders as facilitators'
Organisations & teams as communities where everyone is included
'My castle'
Empowered people
Shared purpose
Agency
Curiosity
Open-mindedness
'Our castle'
Connected teams
Shared purpose
Dynamism
Self-direction
Collective conscious

How to create a sense of belonging at work

Figure 2.1 presents the Five Principles of Belonging in organisations and provides structure for creating a plan (Figure 2.1). At the centre of the model is the representation of the organisation as a community with the four surrounding pillars creating the conditions and activities that can make this happen. There is no one element of the system more or less important than any other – if you are serious about creating a belonging culture, then you have to take a systemic approach. Neglect one element and your efforts elsewhere will be worthless.

Principle one: Organisations and teams as communities where everyone is included

At the centre of the diagram is the core principle of belonging at work (Figure 2.2). A community is an organised social structure where a group of individuals share a mutual concern for one another's welfare. Reframing the organisation as a community gives a sense of 'people first', thus enabling a strong foundation for developing a sense of belonging.

Core characteristics

The organisation as a community is central to a belonging culture and informs the attributes of the surrounding elements. The critical characteristics can be summarised as:

1 The organisation-community provides according to everybody's individual needs and what they need to thrive and grow.

2 The organisation-community protects the well-being and welfare of all employees.

Figure 2.2 Belonging culture: 'Everyone included, everybody thrives'

31

3 Behaviours and values reflect those of society norms and the organisation-community provides the psychological safety for all employees to speak up and address intolerable behaviours.

4 The organisation-community's primary concern is providing an environment where every employee is included, supported, accepted and valued. This creates a level playing-field of opportunity which allows each individual to maximise their talent.

When organisations had to adapt to the majority of their workforces working from home in the early stages of the COVID crisis, leaders became concerned about what this meant for culture, engagement and connectivity.

This is a strong indicator of the, perhaps mistaken, value organisations place on the physical presence of the workplace. Let's think about it from a town or country community perspective. We know that there are many divisions that exist in populations who share the same territory. In addition, there is competition for resources and power. These populations come together when they want to promote the needs of, or defend, the territory. We saw this in action when the majority of businesses, aligned around the shared purpose of keeping the business going in the face of crisis, made unprecedented progress in innovating and adapting in response. The difference was that, on an individual level, people knew that it was in their interest and that of the wider organisation. Each individual felt a sense of meaning and collaborated around a shared purpose.

Most organisations have developed in such a way that they do not enjoy the benefits or reap the rewards of a true community because they fail to focus on creating both meaning and purpose. This meaning and purpose creates a true sense of belonging and connectivity.

In his book *The Art of Community*, Charles H. Vogl describes how these differences manifest by describing four key differences between the average organisation and those where there is a true sense of community:

Organisation	Community
Formal, published values – *the organisation talks the talk*	Implicit values – *everyone walks the walk*
Employees expected to conform to formal and informal standards, practice and behaviours, which may compromise individual values	Membership identity – *I know how I should behave and my work identity doesn't compromise my core identity*
Behaviour frameworks focus on performance and there is little incentive to call out contrary behaviours or actions	Moral proscriptions – *we all protect and respect one another. We share a view of what is intolerable and we address it*

Organisation	Community
Formal processes, such as engagement surveys, attempt to gauge the degree to which employees are committed to the organisation and identify the 'levers' driving or impeding current performance	Insider understanding – *I am valued and understood; there is strong emotional understanding in the organisation that has no need to be articulated. As a result, we consistently strive to achieve great things. If this is compromised, we all feel it and recognise it*

Principle two: Belonging culture – 'Everyone included, everybody thrives'

Culture is, essentially, the social order of the organisation-community informing the attitudes, behaviours and actions of everyone within it. Cultural norms are indicators of what is acceptable and unacceptable, and are significantly more powerful than any behaviour or values framework. In a belonging culture, these norms should align to individual personal values and encourage connectivity between employees. This creates understanding and a sense of shared purpose across the organisation.

Consistency and transparency

- *Consistency:* trust is built upon consistency and the predictability of behaviours and actions. The organisation must engender trust within employees to create psychological safety, energy and engagement around shared purpose. Many organisational cultures suffer due to implicit contradictions between their leadership and actions, which negates the sense of purpose. For example, a shared sense of purpose will be destroyed by authoritarian structures and leadership styles, self-direction will be destroyed by centralised decision making and learning through curiosity will be destroyed by strict bureaucracy. Creating a belonging culture requires examination of the processes and actions that will hamper the effort.
- *Transparency:* clear, consistent, frequent and transparent communication is critical for both developing trust and reinforcing cultural norms. Communication should not be seen as top-down, one-way information dissemination but as prompts to start conversations. The tone should be consistent, familial and human, inviting people to respond and providing the platforms for them to do so. In addition, the organisation should communicate bad news clearly, as well as good. If you are communicating results of the Belonging Audit or an engagement survey, be bold in your message and don't dilute or mask the negative. If there is a glaring issue, share it. Apologise, tell the employees that this is not good enough, that the organisation is committed to improving and share what actions will be taken.

Connectivity

The organisation has a role in establishing systemic connectivity and collaboration, which promotes understanding, creates emotional connectivity to the organisation, creates agile teams and drives innovation. The role is about how these connections are encouraged and facilitated, as well as allowing employees the freedom to connect, collaborate and share across the organisation. Consistent and transparent communication described above should focus on creating open dialogue, which encourages employees to connect with others. The organisation should facilitate a variety of connections based on sharing knowledge, personal interests, innovation and future-thinking, charitable work and experimental projects.

Integrity

In cultures where integrity is implicit, values on the wall are reflected in day-to-day behaviours. There is no 'say–do' gap. Promises made are promises kept, or an explanation given as to why not.

Be clear about the behavioural expectations with staff, recognise desired behaviours, call out undesired behaviours and exit perpetrators of discrimination, bullying and harassment. I hear, far too often, the cry of, 'It isn't as simple as that!' It is. It really is as simple as that. Organisations allow bureaucracy, politics and process to get in the way (or they hide behind them). Integrity is the beating heart of the organisation and, in the organisation-community, toxicity will not be tolerated. Think of it as the conscience of the organisation – that means opening your eyes to where people are not thriving and dealing with it swiftly and purposefully.

Integrity and 'ethical fading'

'The process by which the moral colours of an ethical decision fade into bleached hues that are void of moral implications.'

Ann Tenbrunsel, author and professor

Employees may be prone to self-deception when they see an ethical dilemma primarily as a financial dilemma or personal dilemma instead. For example, this could be fixing figures in a report to protect personal financial stability or treating others without dignity and respect when singularly focused on goal achievement. The integrity of an organisation is compromised in this way when priorities such as shareholder value are reinforced to the extent that it usurps everything else or where there is over-bureaucratic focus on KPIs or performance metrics. This can lead to decision making that compromises the personal values of employees and behaviours and that are contrary to those that create a sense of belonging and purpose.

Organisations should look at how they communicate priorities and look at the processes and systems that foster this behaviour. Ethical fading can be avoided by leaders reframing when problem solving – that is, clearly identifying the ethical implications before focusing on financial or productivity goals.

Principle three: Empowered people – 'My castle'

Overview

Within the context of the organisation, positive self-evaluation confirmed by group interaction, and supported by leaders, gives us a strong work identity that has been positively correlated with:

- commitment to work and organisation
- performance and motivation
- change and transformation
- well-being and happiness
- learning.

'My home is my castle and my safest refuge.'

This phrase sums up how we feel about our personal self. The metaphor of the 'home' suggests a place where we are:

- able to be ourselves
- accepted for who we are without compromise
- in control and have agency
- safe.

If we consider the importance of this saying in the personal identity, in order to create coherence between this and our work self, we must feel a similar sense of control and psychological safety in the workplace. This is why empowerment has to be a critical aspect of employee lived experience and all actions in terms of culture, leadership and teams for your plan should be designed to support this. Empowerment allows each individual to connect emotionally with, and give meaning to, the work that they do.

The role and responsibilities of the individual in a belonging culture

While empowerment and inclusion are supported by leadership, teams and the wider organisation, every employee has a critical role in ensuring that they facilitate and support the empowerment and inclusion of others (Figure 2.3).

Figure 2.3 Empowered people: 'My castle'

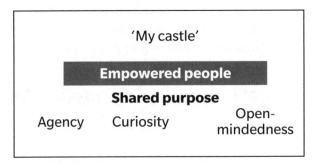

The key attributes within this are:

1 Agency

A sense of agency means to act independently and to make our own free choices. We feel responsible for our actions and their consequences – when somebody has agency, they take ownership and are much less likely to blame others for their mistakes. Agency is critical to empowerment and gives meaning to the things we do. In this way, having a sense of agency means we feel our work has purpose and value, allowing us to feel greater connectivity to a team or organisation.

2 Curiosity

Given how critical innovation has become for organisations, curiosity has come under the spotlight in organisations as an attribute that helps to drive progress. Curiosity is, essentially, the desire 'to know'. However, organisations should not just consider curiosity as something that underpins the creative thinking process because, more importantly, it is also an attribute that fosters connectivity and understanding between people. It is this connectivity that supports a sense of belonging, as well as business-critical innovation, resilience and agility.

3 Open-mindedness

"Pray, don't find fault with the man that limps,
Or stumbles along the road.
Unless you have worn the moccasins he wears,
Or stumbled beneath the same load."

Mary T. Lathrap, *Judge Softly* **(1895)**

Being open-minded is the degree to which an individual is willing to consider a variety of diverse perspectives, values, opinions, or beliefs, even if they contradict your own. Those who are open-minded seek out new experiences and viewpoints, connecting with others and developing understanding. Open-mindedness encourages acceptance of differences, suspends judgement and values the contribution of all. Empathy develops as a result of open-mindedness and has been shown to be a strong predictor of success. As a trait embedded in organisations, it has been shown to increase engagement and foster innovative behaviours. In short, being open-minded makes us behave like good humans – and this is something long overdue as a value in the fabric of organisations.

Open-mindedness is critical in creating a systemic sense of belonging as it promotes understanding, acceptance, collaboration and connectivity between diverse employees. The power of understanding should not be under-estimated in its ability to change attitudes and transform teams.

Seven questions

The entrepreneur and author Seth Godin suggests seven questions we should ask ourselves to understand the degree to which we are open-minded. As you consider each one, test your responses by thinking of specific examples that substantiate your thinking.

1 Do you let the facts get in the way of a good story? When you communicate, do you engage hearts and minds, do you create a narrative beyond your own interpretation of the facts, using stories that show your understanding of the diverse perspectives of others?

2 What do you do with people who disagree with you . . . do you shut them down by dismissing their opinions, inferring you are more qualified to know the right answer?

3 Are you open to multiple points of view or do you demand compliance and uniformity?

4 Is it OK if someone else gets the credit?

5 How often are you able to change your position?

6 Do you have a goal that can be reached in multiple ways?

7 If someone else can get us there faster, are you willing to let them?

What does this tell you about how open-minded others may perceive you to be? Based on your responses to each question, what specifically can you do to foster and reap the rewards of open-mindedness? Some ideas:

• Seek and invite the ideas and opinions of everyone.

• Seek and invite ideas and opinions from a diverse internal network.

• Listen actively *and* actively seek to understand.

• Acknowledge that your own and others' beliefs and filters can be limiting.

- Accept and respect the beliefs, viewpoints and choices of others.
- Develop the ability to see things easily from different perspectives.
- Openly admit to mistakes and communicate what you have learned from them.
- Be open to changing your mind and don't consider it a sign of weakness.

'We failed': creating belonging at LinkedIn

In 2016, Pat Wadors, then vice-president of Global Talent Organization at LinkedIn, wrote in a *Harvard Business Review* article:

'Over the past decade, technology companies and their leaders have launched diversity and inclusion initiatives, hoping to make employees of all backgrounds and experiences feel welcome in our industry. We failed.'

Since then, LinkedIn has shifted its focus to create a sense of belonging within the organisation, understanding that this is the key to creating energy and engagement within the organisation. Activities include:

- Belonging moments: conscious effort and time is given to regularly share stories to create empathy and connectivity within teams.
- Recognising individuality, embracing difference and giving it a voice, 'I hired you because you're different. I hired you to do X and I want your experience at this company. How do I make sure you don't lose your conviction to speak up?'
- Treating people beautifully: leaders and managers are trained to ensure that the onboarding process welcomes the whole individual to the team, not just as somebody employed to execute a set of tasks. This makes people feel valued for who they are and sets the tone for their experience as an employee at LinkedIn.
- 'The Quiet Ambassador' programme designed to recognise the unique voice and value of the introvert versus the extrovert. Leaders are trained in how to bring the best out of introverted team members and how to run their team meetings so that everyone has a voice, 'I'll give you the notes of the meeting and the presentation 24 hours in advance so you have time to sift through and have a point of view by that time. I won't put you on the spot. We'll reduce our brainstorming. We'll have an internet site where you can put in your notes after the meeting.'

Principle four: Identity-centred leadership – 'Leaders as facilitators'

The role of leaders and line managers is absolutely pivotal in creating a sense of belonging and the roles take on a centrality within organisations unprecedented in traditional organisational structures. The shift is long overdue, it being the role that supports belonging by protecting the lived experience of employees, and has been expedited by increased virtual working, the role now being a conduit between the individual, the team and the wider organisation. The leader's role in an organisation-community is not one of 'command and control' but, rather, that of a facilitator meeting the needs of individual talents and creating connectivity in teams (Figure 2.4). The leader has to shift their position in this respect to being 'beside' rather than 'above' the individual and the team.

'Treat your boss like a peer, and your peers like a boss'

Bruce Sewell: Apple's former general counsel

This is one of 'Sewell's Rules', which define his unique and effective approach to leadership. In this rule, he proposes rethinking your relationships in the context of organisations.

'Treat your peers as you would normally treat your boss. And then, by contrast, treat your boss more like a peer . . . It sounds a little odd, but if you back up and analyse it, the things that your peers really need from you are good communication. They need to know that your word is your bond, when you say that you'll deliver some piece of work or that you'll be a team member that you'll show up, you're there.

'That mindset helps ensure that decisions aren't made in isolation. Leaders benefit because it enables them to more effectively shape attitudes within the company, while the team members will be entrusted with more responsibilities, ensuring a more cohesive, productive and effective organizational culture.'

Figure 2.4 Identity-centred leadership: 'Leaders as facilitators'

Curiosity	Courage	Humanity
	Shared purpose	
	Identity-centred leadership	
	'Leaders as facilitators'	

Curiosity

Curiosity is a core aspect of being human and is, in fact, one of the oldest cognitive pathways we have. As explained earlier, our primitive instinct to be curious is often stifled by the corporate environment and discouraged where there is strict hierarchy or siloed teams. Within the organisation-community, where effort is made for these barriers to be lifted, the identity-centred leader should develop a curious mindset to leverage team relationships, drive motivation, foster innovation and role model the behaviours to encourage team members to do the same.

Plato said, 'Learning is, by nature, curiosity.' The most successful leaders are those who never stop learning and, as a result, are able to make new connections between people and things. A curious mindset where a leader is constantly looking for new information and reframing what already exists means they can truly embrace the recurring disruption within which organisations today must constantly re-invent or die. Being curious has to be done authentically, free of typical 'leadership development' frameworks. At times, it may look chaotic, slightly maverick and eccentric. But then, isn't that how the best leaders and pioneers tend to be?

Being curious helps a leader to demonstrate empathy and develop understanding of each of the team members. Getting to know each individual really well fosters trust and a sense of belonging. In addition, this knowledge helps the leader to leverage individual talent by tapping into specific strengths and helping each team member to develop and grow in the direction that they choose. Giving regular time to ask questions and listen to each team member also ensures that the leader is able to monitor well-being and wellness. The team members will feel valued and supported, a sense of deep belonging within the team 'family'.

Teams led by leaders who have a curious mindset and encourage the same in others tend to be motivated, energised and feel a binding sense of purpose. Teams like this are an unstoppable force. They constantly ask, 'Why?' or, 'How can we do this better?' They never give up, but they are more than happy to change direction. They aren't afraid to say, 'I don't know,' but they will always put energy behind finding out. They challenge outside and inside the team, engaging in healthy conflict within problem solving that serves to deepen the connections between team members. They move forward with purpose. They over-achieve. They innovate. They have fun. And they all behave like individual human beings, not employees conforming to a prescribed set of behaviours.

How are you curious?
Five types of curiosity

Todd B. Kashdan and his colleagues at George Mason University have developed a five-dimensional model of curiosity along with a questionnaire that measures each of the dimensions:

1 *Deprivation sensitivity:* those who recognise a gap in their knowledge and feel compelled to fill it.

2 *Joyous exploration:* those who have a constant fascination with the world around them and the hunger to learn about it.

3 *Social curiosity:* talking, listening, observing, being interested in and asking questions about others in order to understand why they think, feel or do the things they do.

4 *Stress tolerance:* a willingness to adapt to or embrace the anxiety that comes with trying out new things or taking risks.

5 *Thrill seeking:* taking risks in novel experiences in order to create thorough understanding of and reinterpretation of complex problems.

Use this scale to indicate the degree to which the following statements describe you:

1 Does not describe me at all.

2 Very slightly describes me.

3 Somewhat describes me.

4 Neutral.

5 Generally describes me.

6 Mostly describes me.

7 Completely describes me.

▶

Deprivation sensitivity

Thinking about solutions to different conceptual problems can keep me awake at night	
I can spend hours on a single problem because I just can't rest without knowing the answer	
I feel frustrated if I can't figure out the solution to a problem, so I work even harder to solve it	
I work relentlessly at problems that I feel must be solved	
It frustrates me to not have all the information I need	
Total	

Joyous exploration

I view challenging situations as an opportunity to grow and learn	
I am always looking for experiences that challenge how I think about myself and the world	
I seek out situations where it is likely that I will have to think in depth about something	
I enjoy learning about subjects that are unfamiliar to me	
I find it fascinating to learn new information	
Total	

Social curiosity

I like to learn about the habits of others	
I like finding out why people behave the way they do	
When other people are having a conversation, I like to find out what it's about	
When around other people, I like listening to their conversations	
When people argue, I like to know what is going on	
Total	

Stress tolerance

The smallest doubt can stop me from seeking out new experiences	
I cannot handle stress that comes from entering uncertain situations	
I find it hard to explore new places when I lack confidence in my abilities	
I cannot function well if I am unsure whether a new experience is safe	
It is difficult to concentrate when there is a possibility that I will be taken by surprise	
Total	

Thrill seeking

The anxiety of doing something new makes me feel excited and alive	
Risk taking is exciting to me	
When I have free time, I want to do things that are a little scary	
Creating an adventure as I go is much more appealing than a planned adventure	
I prefer friends who are excitingly unpredictable	
Total	

Scoring: Add up your score for each dimension, reverse scoring for stress tolerance (e.g. 'Does not describe me at all' scores 7, 'Completely describes me' scores 1)

Interpretation (calculated using a US national representative sample)

Deprivation sensitivity	Joyous exploration	Social curiosity	Stress tolerance	Thrill seeking
Low: <3.7 Med: ≥ 4.9 High: >6.0	Low: <4.1 Med: ≥ 5.2 High: >6.3	Low: <3.0 Med: ≥ 4.4 High: >5.8	Low: <3.1 Med: ≥ 4.4 High: >5.8	Low: <2.6 Med: ≥ 3.9 High: >5.2

What do your results mean?

We have explored the importance of curiosity as a core attribute of the identity-centred leader. You should consider the implications of your scores with regard to:

- What aspects of curiosity do I role model to the team?
- Which aspects am I least likely to role model?
- What are the implications?

Examples:

- If you score high on deprivation sensitivity, how does this impact the team? The upside is that the team can rely on you to solve problems on their behalf, but could you potentially prevent them from solving problems?
- If you score high on joyous exploration, do you see this energy reflected in your team? If not, how could you harness this?
- If you score low on social curiosity, how can you increase this to ensure you create the psychological safety for others to do the same as well as to demonstrate curiosity in getting to know each of your team members?
- If your stress tolerance is low, could this impact how empowered your team members feel? Could they be mirroring your risk aversion?
- If your thrill-seeking score is high, how can you use this to encourage others to take risks, but ensure that it remains within reasonable parameters?

Courage

Courage is demonstrated when a leader consciously decides on an action that has never been tried before, which may contradict popular opinion, disregard an established process or method or perhaps call out the behaviour of others that conflicts with organisational or personal leadership values, because they believe it is the 'right' thing to do. They are comfortable with being uncomfortable and they are not afraid to show vulnerability, owning their mistakes or weaknesses. When a leader consistently acts with courage, they trust in and develop the trust of those around them.

Courageous leaders tend to engender trust in those around them and inspire employees to go above and beyond in their efforts. Acting with courage allows leaders to experiment and take risks, encouraging their teams to do the same, creating agile and innovative teams. The passion of courageous leaders creates cohesion and energy in teams – employees feel strongly motivated and determined to work together towards performance excellence. This type of leadership creates almost a familial bond between the leader and team.

Leading with courage is a game changer for organisations wanting to create a sense of community and belonging. If leaders are afraid of speaking up and calling out what they intrinsically believe to be right or wrong, the organisation-community comes tumbling down.

It is critical that this courage is echoed by the executive team – that they are willing to hold one another accountable and call out anything that contradicts the purpose and values of the organisation. They should find opportunities to demonstrate this courage publicly – to use no-nonsense language and talk about what is important to them personally. They need to show vulnerability by expressing feelings, sharing weaknesses and sometimes saying, 'I don't know.'

Humanity

'If your actions inspire others to dream more, learn more, do more and become more, you are a leader.'

Simon Sinek, author

Now is the right time to bring the human element back into the heart of organisations. Cut out the bureaucracy, quit hiding behind corporate speak, stop relying on processes and frameworks and start leading with humanity. Leading with humanity means leading with your heart as well as your head and putting people first, in all circumstances, without exception. Enough is enough. The management theories that gathered pace from the 1960s have led organisations to become pseudo-worlds where numbers, processes, models, frameworks, 'paradigms', plans and data are so entrenched that their purpose is rarely questioned and employees are fitted around these elements with everyone kidding themselves that this is the best way to create high performance. If the majority of leadership models are to be believed, leaders need only adapt their approach according to a prescribed four-box grid to lead motivated, engaged and high-performing teams. (Note: I haven't missed the irony of the fact that I am forcefully dismissing all of these things while I am writing a book about organisations and leadership, which includes my own model! I hope it is understood that the model I propose here is to help organisations understand that it really is possible to let everybody be a self-directed individual, to create a community where everyone belongs and still succeed financially.)

Organisations are merely a group of people who (mostly) find it easy enough to be decent human beings in the external world but somehow lose the know-how when navigating the maze of 'stuff' that overcomplicates what should really be pretty simple. So, my leadership advice is thus:

Be a good human being. Always.

Pithy as it may sound, having this as a mantra for your leadership focus will lead you to significantly greater success and happiness than any four-box grid model. Leading with humanity means treating everybody as an individual and valuing them for who they are not just what they do. Be compassionate and ensure that everyone feels included. Recognise that behaviours are more complex than they outwardly appear, so, rather than judge, consider the other person's circumstances and seek to understand.

Leading with humanity means leading with purpose – and authority is the enemy of purpose. Don't exert power over people unless circumstance genuinely requires it – a job title doesn't give anyone the right to control another person. Walk alongside people, be humble, don't be judgemental and be kind.

Leading with humanity in the organisation-community means frequently asking:

'How can I make your life better?'

Principle five: Connected teams – 'Our castle'

'Connection is an intuitive sense of belonging. Connection is the difference between I am and we are.'

Ari Kopoulos, CEO, EmployeeConnect

Extending the castle metaphor from earlier, connected teams create environments in which we are:

* able to be ourselves
* accepted for who we are without compromise
* in control and have agency
* safe.

Connectivity and diversity in teams are critical to innovation and agility. However, teams are more than just the sum of their parts, which is why connectivity is both challenging and critical. If we consider a team of 7 people, there are:

* 21 sets of pairs
* 35 sets of 3 people
* 35 sets of 4 people
* 21 sets of 5 people

Figure 2.5 Connected teams: 'Our castle'

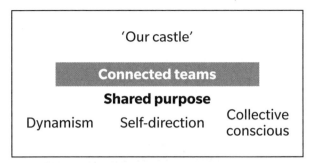

- 7 sets of 6 people
- 1 set of 7 people
- 120 sets of relationships!

With this in mind, a sense of purpose as the central source of connection within a team is absolutely paramount (Figure 2.5). The characteristics of teams that create shared purpose are shaped largely by the attributes of the identity-centred leader, they depend on the attributes defined under 'empowered people' and, to a lesser degree, are influenced by the wider system. By building strong relationships with all team members, the leader is more able to navigate this relational complexity.

When teams have a shared sense of purpose, they develop emotional connections which create 'affective trust', genuine feelings of concern and care, rather than just 'cognitive trust', understanding that someone has the competence to do their job. This is the fundamental difference between teams who create transformation and those who merely transact.

Dynamism

Dynamism in teams is characterised by awareness of individual/team performance and continually adapting in response to performance, customer need, crisis and external environment. The leader's role in this is similar to that of the cox in rowing – coaching, steering, executing strategy, keeping the team synchronised, focusing passionately on the goal and creating the energy the team need to relentlessly pursue it.

Where there is shared purpose, teams will recognise when one member is unable to commit all their energy to performance, closing the gap and remaining concerned about their team mate's welfare until they are ready to get back on track. The leader encourages this by offering support and focusing on the collective goals of the team rather than the temporary decline in the individual's performance.

Research has shown that teams like this thrive and raise performance in the face of external threat – given the disruptive and constantly fluctuating environment businesses operate within today, this must surely be the number-one priority for all team leaders.

Self-direction

The main aspect of self-direction in this context is the collective contribution to decision making and direction. This means the leader's choice is equal to all other team members, their role being to ensure the team has all the resources and information they need, offering their ideas, insights and experience as a contribution. From a governance perspective, there are clearly exceptions to this – what organisations need to ask themselves is whether there are too many exceptions being driven by power boundaries and hierarchy.

In order for self-direction to be effective, it does require the group to adhere to a set of standards that they have collectively agreed. Think of this like 'House Rules'. Everyone has a voice and a contribution to make, but core team principles can help to prevent unnecessary conflict. For example:

- We are fully present.
- We respect boundaries.
- We challenge our assumptions and biases, as well as those of our colleagues.
- We are constantly curious.
- We are open to feeling uncomfortable.
- Looking after one another is our main priority.

The team should expand the meaning of each of the principles, identify the how and provide specific indicators for contrary behaviours.

Collective consciousness

Collective consciousness in a team is the shared beliefs, ideas, attitudes and knowledge that develops around a shared sense of purpose. It is consolidated by the leader's facilitation of connectivity previously discussed and informs the sense of belonging within an identity of the team.

For a long time, it was assumed that the comparatively large size of the human brain evolved in order to process facts and information about the world around us. However, later evolutionary theories assert that our brains evolved in this way so that we could deal with the complexity of groups and social interactions. We uniquely differ from other primates because we have the ability to share our intentions with others and jointly pursue goals. Our brains were literally built for collaboration. We don't have enough brain space to be the expert on everything and we need to collaborate with others in order to be able to successfully apply our own knowledge. Consider medical pathways:

- You make an appointment with a doctor via a receptionist because you have a problem with your knee.
- The doctor refers you to a medical specialist.
- The specialist's secretary contacts you to arrange the appointment.
- You arrive for your appointment and are first seen by a nurse who runs some general tests.
- These tests are sent to the laboratory where they are processed by lab staff and then given to the specialist.
- The specialist does his assessment, refers to the test results and decides that you need surgery to correct the problem.
- The specialist's secretary makes the relevant arrangements for the surgery to be scheduled and contacts you regarding the date of the surgery.
- On the day, you are given a pre-med by a nurse, settled into a ward by another nurse, visited by both the anaesthetist and the surgeon prior to the surgery.
- You are taken up to the operating theatre by a hospital porter and greeted by a theatre nurse who prepares you for the anaesthetic.
- The surgery is completed by the surgeon, anaesthetist, two other surgeons and two nurses.
- The surgery is a success and you tell everyone you meet about this amazing surgeon who fixed your knee . . .

Do you get the picture? Without all the other people, the surgeon would never have been able to apply his skills and you would probably still be limping.

In short, we are significantly smarter as a group than we are as individuals.

Why, then, do organisations focus on assessing and rewarding individual performance? They seem to believe that, by throwing a few generic collaboration statements into a behaviour framework, they have the issue covered.

Your organisation as a community

Take a look at the characteristics of organisations and communities and consider these within the context of your own organisation or team.

Consider the questions in any engagement or inclusion surveys, or any other data points, that could help you to assess the degree to which the lived experience of employees reflects the characteristics of communities.

With regard to each of the descriptors, where on the scale below would you estimate your team or organisation sit?

Organisation	Community
Formal, published values – *the organisation talks the talk*	Implicit values – *everyone walks the walk*

Organisation	Neutral	Community
100%	0%	100%

Employees expected to conform to formal and informal standards, practice and behaviours, which may compromise individual values	Membership identity – *I know how I should behave and my work identity doesn't compromise my core identity*

Organisation	Neutral	Community
100%	0%	100%

Behaviour frameworks focus on performance and there is little incentive to call out contrary behaviours or actions	Moral proscriptions – *we all protect and respect one another. We share a view of what is intolerable and we address it*

Organisation	Neutral	Community
100%	0%.	100%

Formal processes, such as engagement surveys, attempt to gauge the degree to which employees are committed to the organisation and identify the 'levers' driving or impeding current performance	Insider understanding – *I am valued and understood; there is strong emotional understanding in the organisation that has no need to be articulated. As a result, we consistently strive to achieve great things. If this is compromised, we all feel it and recognise it*

Organisation	Neutral	Community
100%	0%	100%

- Which aspects of your team or organisation are most like a community? What evidence do you have?
- Which are most like an organisation? What evidence do you have?
- What information is missing? What else would you like to know?

This information will help to inform the questions you ask in the Belonging Audit, which we will cover in the next chapter.

part 2

How to create
a sense of
belonging

chapter 3

Carry out the Belonging Audit

To start building a belonging culture, you need to know where you are now – the more time and effort invested in this, the more compelling the business case will be. In this chapter, I will guide you through the process of planning, doing and reviewing a Belonging Audit, as well as give tips for how the exercise can be adapted for teams and smaller businesses (under 50 employees).

Before you begin

Before you embark on a Belonging Audit, there are two key things you should consider:

1 Appetite for inconvenient truths

This process may uncover some unexpected issues or 'elephants in the room' that are unpalatable for some organisations. It is important to ensure that the senior leadership team are prepared to understand and address any challenging insights that present. If there is no appetite for addressing anything that arises, then conducting the audit and not acting on the information could disengage those who are marginalised even further.

2 Timing

As with any initiative, to ensure engagement with the survey and subsequent success of the programme, the timing must be right. Any activity that may be causing negative morale, anxiety or engagement in the organisation, such as a merger or potential redundancies, could impact the responses to the survey and lead to developing a plan that doesn't necessarily address the implicit issues.

Belonging Audit: planning

1 Creating the project plan

Ensure that you have a robust project plan so that it is easy to manage and everyone understands their role. The plan should at least include:

- Planning:
  - Identifying and engaging support
  - Identifying a platform to deliver a survey
  - Creating the survey.
- Doing:
  - Engaging the audience and delivering the survey.
- Reviewing:
  - Analysing the data.

2 Identifying and engaging support

Depending on the size of the team or organisation and your role, you may need to involve others in doing the audit and get their buy-in as to why you are taking this approach. At this point, you are not building the business case for belonging, simply helping those involved to understand why you want to conduct the audit. At the least, you would probably want to consider engaging:

- a leadership sponsor to endorse the project (if it is not you)
- HR
- a data analyst, either internal or external, if you do not have someone suitable in-house. In smaller businesses where there is significantly less data, you could pair up with a colleague to do the analysis
- an assistant or colleague who can manage the process.

When engaging those from whom you are requesting support, create a simple, consistent narrative to explain why you want to do the Belonging Audit and to make sure everyone is on the same page. For example, something along the lines of:

'Research has shown that belonging is the key indicator of inclusion in an organisation, with many organisations focusing on this rather than traditional top-down D&I efforts, which have had relatively poor impact. It would be interesting to find out the degree to which all of our employees feel a sense of belonging.'

3 Identifying a platform to deliver a survey

In larger organisations, you may want to use an external agency to deliver the process. Whether externally or internally delivered, while there will always be some people suspicious of data and unwilling to take part, a promise of and commitment to complete anonymity will certainly encourage more people to complete the survey. If you think people in your organisation will be particularly cautious about engaging with the process, ask yourself why and consider what messages you will need to give to encourage participation.

Some survey agencies provide a completely bespoke end-to-end service, but, if you are keeping it in-house, there are many online platforms such as SurveyMonkey where you can create, deliver and analyse your survey.

Belonging Audit: doing

1 Engaging the participants

Consider asking your leadership sponsor to put his name to the launch message, if you think it will increase engagement. As with any survey, it is important to prepare the audience for the survey by communicating positive messages as to its purpose. Crafting a message that signals the positive goal of wanting to understand the extent to which people feel like they belong in the organisation, the anonymity of the survey and the intention of wanting to use the results to improve the employee experience for *all* employees, will likely increase engagement across all groups. There is growing D&I/engagement survey fatigue in organisations where they have found there to be few positive changes as a result. This message signals an inclusive, no-jargon, personal approach, which should help to drive engagement with the initiative – if only, at this early stage, out of curiosity.

2 Creating the survey

If you wish to create a bespoke questionnaire, most survey platforms have lots of guidance for dos and don'ts when doing so, considering things such as survey length, formulating questions, response scales and open answer questions. To make sure you create a survey that delivers the insights you are looking for, do your research before you begin.

While it is good to follow expert advice from a platform or agent, it is critical that a belonging survey *feels* different. It shouldn't have all the usual questions included in engagement or D&I surveys that will deliver the same responses without providing insight into the real issues and opportunities. By all means, use some of the questions from survey banks, but add in some questions that feel different. Questions that will make people sit up and understand that, this time, you mean business.

Consider the exercises from Chapters 1 and 2 ('Perception gap' and 'Your organisation as a community').

- What lived experience data are you missing?
- What else would you like to find out about the felt sense of belonging or the sense of community in your organisation?
- What questions might provide lived experience insight into the success of any current D&I initiatives?

The 'Belonging Audit questionnaire' below is a good starting point that you can use as it is or adapt, according to the insights gained from your analysis. It includes a demographics questionnaire that you can adapt according to your location, culture, team/organisation size and the key insights you are looking for. The list included here is extensive, providing the greatest insight regarding the experiences of specific intersectional identities, but may not be suitable where there are less people so could, potentially, remove anonymity.

Engagement with the process has to ensure that the respondent feels in control so, you should make it clear that there is no obligation to answer any of the questions. Where respondents don't answer this in itself is useful information when it comes to the analysis.

Belonging Audit questionnaire

Welcome to the Belonging Audit questionnaire. Your responses and information are securely and anonymously collected so, please be as open and honest as you can in completing this survey. There are 16 multiple

---

choice questions where you are asked to indicate the degree to which you agree or disagree with a statement. In addition, there are two open questions where you can provide more specific data that can help us to understand more about positive or negative experiences impacting belonging in our organisation.

We want to ensure that everyone in the organisation feels that they belong so, knowing broadly who does or doesn't can help us to focus activities in the right areas. For that reason, we have included some demographic questions at the end of the survey to ensure that we focus energy and resource towards the areas in which it will be of greatest benefit.

Please enter your function/business unit:

1 Being an employee here does not require me to relinquish my values or principles.
Strongly agree – agree – neither agree nor disagree – disagree – strongly disagree

2 I use 'we/us' rather than 'they/them' when I refer to my organisation externally.
Strongly agree – agree – neither agree nor disagree – disagree – strongly disagree

3 I am often treated in a way that makes me feel ashamed, inferior, unimportant or excluded.
Strongly agree – agree – neither agree nor disagree – disagree – strongly disagree

4 I often witness behaviours or actions which appear to make somebody feel ashamed, inferior, unimportant or excluded.
Strongly agree – agree – neither agree nor disagree – disagree – strongly disagree

5 Everyone in the organisation belongs – there are no extremes of privilege or disadvantage.
Strongly agree – agree – neither agree nor disagree – disagree – strongly disagree

6 If I see someone being treated in a way I find unacceptable from a respect or moral perspective, I always feel comfortable about 'calling it out'.
Strongly agree – agree – neither agree nor disagree – disagree – strongly disagree

▶

7 In work, I am happy more often than I experience negative emotion.
Strongly agree – agree – neither agree nor disagree – disagree – strongly disagree

8 I sometimes feel scared, sad, insecure or alone here.
Strongly agree – agree – neither agree nor disagree – disagree – strongly disagree

9 I feel like I belong here and it inspires me to go above and beyond what is expected.
Strongly agree – agree – neither agree nor disagree – disagree – strongly disagree

10 Leaders here are committed to ensuring that everyone feels that they belong here.
Strongly agree – agree – neither agree nor disagree – disagree – strongly disagree

11 I feel accepted and respected here for all aspects of my identity and who I am.
Strongly agree – agree – neither agree nor disagree – disagree – strongly disagree

12 My individual needs are well met by my organisation.
Strongly agree – agree – neither agree nor disagree – disagree – strongly disagree

13 There is a feeling of collective responsibility for the welfare and well-being of everyone in the organisation.
Strongly agree – agree – neither agree nor disagree – disagree – strongly disagree

14 In the last 12 months, I feel that my health, well-being or general happiness has been impacted negatively by experiences at work.
Strongly agree – agree – neither agree nor disagree – disagree – strongly disagree

15 I am optimistic about the future in most aspects of my life.
Strongly agree – agree – neither agree nor disagree – disagree – strongly disagree

16 I am valued here.
Strongly agree – agree – neither agree nor disagree – disagree – strongly disagree

Are there any specific positive experiences you would like to share that have impacted your sense of belonging (without using names)?

Are there any specific negative experiences you would like to share that have impacted your sense of belonging (without using names)?

Please answer the following questions:

Gender identity

Non-binary/non-conforming
Man
Woman
Other; please specify:

Do you identify as transgender?

No
Yes

Sexual orientation

Bisexual
Gay/lesbian
Heterosexual
Queer
Other; please specify:

Family status

No children
Partnered parent/legal guardian
Single parent/legal guardian

Are you a carer?

No
Yes

Are you a person with a disability?

I have a visible disability
I have an invisible disability
I have both a visible and invisible disability
I do not have a disability

Native language

The primary business language spoken here is:
My native language
Not my native language

Age

<18
18–24
25–34
35–44
45–54
55–64
65+

Time in the organisation

<3 months
3–6 months
6–12 months
1–2 years
2–4 years
4–6 years
6–10 years
10+ years

What is the highest education level you have attained?

Secondary/high school
Vocational training, diploma
Undergraduate degree
Postgraduate degree, doctorate
(Amend according to local education system)

Race/ethnicity UK

Asian
Black
Mixed
White
Other

Most survey tools have the functionality to use rating scale question types, which allow you to assign custom weights to answer choices. This means that you can use the scale above but indicate in the tool which answers indicate positive/negative responses (for example, strongly agree may indicate a positive response on some questions and a negative response on others).

3 Delivering the survey

Give participants sufficient time to respond but not too long that it drops off their radar. The recommended amount of time is normally 10 days, but you may want to increase this over holiday periods. You may want to give participants a couple of friendly reminders before the close to encourage good take-up. A good completion rate is about 81 per cent so, this would be a reasonable target to aim for.

Belonging Audit: reviewing

1 Analysing the data

You can cut the qualitative data in many different ways to identify exactly where the belonging hotspots and coldspots are. Survey platforms provide extensive guidance on how to cut data and do different analyses, if you are not working with a dedicated data analyst. Be curious and look for ways of cutting the data to provide insights such as:

- Which functions/areas of the organisation have the strongest and weakest sense of belonging?
- Which demographic qualities experience the strongest and weakest sense of belonging?
- Which demographic intersections experience the strongest and weakest sense of belonging?
- What is the impact on those who feel that they don't belong?
- Is there a correlation between well-being, health, happiness and optimism responses and a sense of belonging?
- Where is there greater confidence to speak up in defence of others who are marginalised? How is the well-being and happiness in these areas?

Responses to the open-ended questions add depth and narrative to the quantitative insights. Most survey platforms provide ways to analyse qualitative data, by creating categories and sub-categories of themes. So, now I will provide guidance to get creative, dig deep and keep searching for the critical insights that will help you to truly build a picture of the state of belonging in your organisation's culture.

2 Cutting the data

For this, you will need to gather all existing data sources and bring them together with the Belonging Audit data. The more time you spend in data analysis here, the more compelling the business case will be and the more likely you will be to develop a programme that makes a lasting difference to your organisation.

Data sources, which we looked at in Chapter 1, may include, but are not limited to:

- recruitment data
- career progression data
- exit data
- absence data
- flexible working data
- engagement surveys
- inclusion surveys
- pulse surveys
- D&I focus groups
- employee networks
- performance data
- external D&I benchmarks
- salary data
- employee brand data
- absence data
- well-being data
- grievance data.

In addition, if available, you should gather information on D&I and well-being initiatives currently or recently rolled out:

D&I initiative	KPI	Cost	Well-being initiative	KPI	Cost

Start with the Belonging Audit data

As we have covered, online survey platforms have tools available that will allow you to analyse and cut data. First, you will group the average response for each question into three categories (the systems normally do this for you):

- Good
- Neutral
- Poor.

Then, you will run an analysis of the key themes from the verbatim questions. If the system you are using doesn't allow you to do this, there are many free word cloud generators online that can help you to do this. Take the top three of:

- Positive verbatim themes

  1

  2

  3

- Negative verbatim themes

  1

  2

  3

Now, you will cut the data to include the demographic data and look for correlations between demographic groups and question responses. This is where you start to understand who does and who doesn't feel a sense of belonging in the organisation. To do this:

1 Calculate the response rate to see how many employees completed the survey.

2 Generate a list of demographic data to understand the proportional representation of the respondents (this is also interesting to understand the intersectional identities in the organisation).

3 Now, for each question, you can run an analysis to see the demographic differences between the question responses.

4 Bringing this data together, you will be able to see which demographics gave the most and least favourable responses.

Now, move to the data you don't have and what you want to know

Start with a list of questions to which you would like the answers, to understand the impact on those who feel that they don't belong. Here are a few you may want to start with:

- What does recruitment data tell you about the demographics of those employed over the last 12 months? Which demographics were most likely to be rejected in the recruitment process?
- What does exit data tell you about who is most likely to leave the organisation? What proportion of the overall organisation do the top demographics represent? If you have exit data, what is the main reason for employees leaving?
- What does absence data tell you about who is most likely to miss work due to illness? What proportion of the overall organisation do these demographics represent? What is the average salary in these demographics?
- What does career progression data tell you about those who are most likely to be promoted? What are the proportionate representations of each demographic (including intersections from the survey data)?
- What is the average tenure for each demographic? What about performance ratings?
- Are there pockets in the organisation that are significantly different from others? In terms of demographic representation, for example, or absence?

Keep going. Dig deep. Get creative. Some analyses may not present particularly useful information, but, leaving no stone unturned, you will be sure to find a few gems and be able to build a narrative of what is really happening in the organisation.

Next, take a look at the qualitative data from the verbatim questions:

- What are the main key themes/words that came up using word clouds?
- How do the key words differ between those who feel that they do belong and those that don't?
- What experiences of belonging, positive and negative, did people describe? Select a few of each that are the most impactful.

What does the data from this tell you about D&I current activities?

Look back to the D&I data regarding current initiatives. What does the data you have analysed tell you about the success of these initiatives? For example, if you have been focusing on attracting and recruiting more ethnic minority talent, and the KPI was representation, how does the lived experience of these groups compare to the reported progress of the initiative? Doing this analysis will show you where initiatives really are – or aren't – creating return on investment.

In addition, you can then analyse the financial losses associated with those demographics who feel the least sense of belonging. Bringing all these analyses together, you can start to identify the greatest opportunities and risks, which are the basis for building your plan:

1 Hotspots: list the top five areas where there is a strong sense of belonging.

2 Coldspots: list the top five areas that indicate a poor sense of belonging.

3 What are the opportunities to drive progress or leverage current strengths?

4 What are the key risks you can identify from the data analysis?

chapter 4

Build your Belonging Plan

Now that you have undertaken the Belonging Audit and identified the risks and opportunities, this chapter will guide you through the process of building a Belonging Plan and covers:

- how to articulate the themes of your plan based on the analysis you did in Chapter 3
- understanding how to create a vision that has strong purpose
- discovering how the Belonging Framework can help you to identify activities to include in your plan
- bringing it all together and structuring your plan

First, articulate the themes

Your plan should be designed to address the risks and opportunities identified in Chapter 3. These should be articulated clearly as the problem you are looking to solve or the opportunity you are trying to maximise. Keep it simple, but make sure each one is clear and precise. For example:

'We have a significant under-representation of women of colour in technology roles and, in addition, those that are in the role have significantly lower belonging scores and rates of attendance than their peers. We must attract, retain and support career progress of this group within the relevant functions.

'At graduate level, we have focused on recruiting from a diverse talent pool and, at this level, belonging scores are high. The data shows that, at director level, this diversity declines sharply and those in minority groups report a significant drop in a sense of belonging. We must support the career progress of minority groups between graduate and director levels, and address the cultural issues that are affecting their experience as a director.'

This is the first place where your plan will significantly diverge from traditional D&I plans and here is why:

Your themes and plan should not be aligned to business priorities.

To align to business priorities is contradictory to the essence of belonging. Belonging is an unwavering fundamental human need. If we don't feel it, we don't function well. The organisation's responsibility for its employees is fixed and should not change in response to business priorities or high-profile media stories. If you want a happy, healthy, innovative and productive workforce, prioritisation of ensuring that all employees feel a sense of belonging in the organisation should be immune to changes in business objectives or external events.

Then, define your vision

Before you embark on doing any further assessment or even think about starting to construct a plan, I can't tell you how absolutely critical it is to develop a purposeful vision.

Here is my first piece of advice to help you get started. Chuck out the strategic planning rule book. It has long been in need of an update and much of the activity is pointless, fruitless and has lacklustre outcomes. Take a look at every organisation that publishes a D&I vision (or diversity statement, or whatever they want to call it, in an effort to differentiate themselves) and you will probably see phrases such as:

'We aim to maximise the power of diversity and inclusion to drive superior business results.'

What is wrong with this? First of all, 'aim' is a dreadfully mediocre word and smacks of 'apologies if we miss . . .'. Second, if the only reason you think you should hop on board this bandwagon is for business performance, then you should probably stop your aiming now.

> **'We foster an inclusive environment that leverages the diverse backgrounds and perspectives of all of our employees.'**

What is wrong with this? First, how exactly does the organisation do this? Without explanation, it is merely an uninspiring, vanilla, hackneyed collection of words.

Many leaders and organisations talk about how their vision and values are the foundation stones of their organisations. No. They aren't. We all know that. For the large part, vision and values are created with several people in a room being facilitated by a consultant who manages to establish 'consensus' in the group to a set of generic, vanilla words. Vision and values have to be shared and emerge organically in a community. They simply cannot work when imposed top down. Ask anyone outside your HR or comms team if they know what the vision and values are. Ask your team. Indeed, if you are the CEO, in your next meeting, ask the board members . . .

If you want to create a statement about belonging and inclusion that has substance, you have to be brave and break free from the expensive lip service approaches. Speak to human beings, consider all that has been discussed so far in this book. We all live in the same world and we all know what is happening around us, so acknowledge and tell your audience what is important to you and what you are doing about it.

Compare the statements above with that of the domain registrar and web-hosting company GoDaddy:

> **'A Culture of Creativity is life at GoDaddy. We hire the best, give them first-class training and set them loose. If you're driven to perform, you'll fit right in. We approach our work fearlessly, learn quickly, improve constantly, and celebrate our wins at every turn. Everyone is welcome – as an inclusive workplace, our employees are comfortable bringing their authentic whole selves to work. Be you.'**

The tone has character, the language is non-corporate and no-nonsense. It uses the words 'you' and 'our' as much as 'we', signalling the importance of the individual and belonging. The phrase 'set them loose' creates a strong visual indication of empowerment and the final two-word sentence is a bold assertion of respect for individual identity. I like it. But could it go further? Could it be bolder and say what *isn't* welcome in the organisation?

Think along the lines of:

'When you join our organisation, you belong here and are given all that you need to be the best you possibly can be from day one. We hire people because they are unique. And we value uniqueness. "Everyone" here includes everyone else – it is our moral duty as human beings in a shared community to do so. No one, anywhere, has the right to jeopardise the growth, progress, happiness or well-being of another person. In our organisation, we have zero tolerance for any behaviour or action that does so. We want you to be happy, be the best you can be and be you.'

I am sure many of you are looking at this and thinking '*Really*?' But yes, really. If you feel that way because some of the wording doesn't work for your organisation then, sure, develop something that reflects your language. If you are reeling because of the sentiment, then you really have to ask if you are ready for this.

If you are going to put out a statement, make sure it makes clear, in no uncertain terms that employees' well-being, growth and performance are paramount and will be protected at all costs. Make statements that are purposeful, actionable and ambitious. Stick your neck out and declare your organisation's line in the sand publicly.

Your vision will be the yardstick against which you test and measure the impact of your plan.

Now, use the Belonging Framework to identify actions

The Belonging Framework incorporates the principles outlined in Part 1 and provides structure for creating a plan (Figure 4.1). At the centre of the framework is the representation of the organisation as a community, with the surrounding elements creating the conditions and activities that can make this happen. There is no one element of the system more or less important than any other – if you are serious about creating a belonging culture, then you have to take a systemic approach. Neglect one element and your efforts elsewhere will be worthless.

Figure 4.1 The Five Principles of Belonging

Consistency &
transparency   Connectivity   Integrity   Curiosity   Courage   Humanity

Belonging culture   **Identity-centred leadership**

'Everyone included,   'Leaders as facilitators'
everybody thrives'

                    **Organisations & teams as
                    communities where everyone is
                    included**

'My castle'   'Our castle'

Empowered people   **Connected teams**

Agency   Curiosity   Open-   Dynamism   Self-direction   Collective
                       mindedness   conscious

Principle one: Organisations and teams as communities where everyone is included

When assessing what you can do within your organisation or team in terms of building the characteristics of a community, first consider the following:

- Where are you currently on the scale between organisation and community (as assessed in the exercise in Chapter 2 along with the additional insights from the Belonging Audit)?
- Is there an appetite or need for a radical change of culture?
- How big is the team or organisation? Larger corporates may need to take an interactive approach through an extensive transformation programme, while start-ups and growing small businesses have the luxury of building the community from the ground up.
- The percentage of virtual working in the organisation and the estimated percentage in the future. The organisation-community focuses on developing the sense of community around people, outside of a central location, and could be critical to maintaining performance, culture and a sense of belonging in our increasingly virtual world.

Who should lead on belonging and community?

You should think very carefully about where the lead team sits within the organisation. Again, consideration must be given to the size of the organisation, but, as far as possible, the team should be self-led and autonomous if it is truly to reflect the essence of community. Though it may be fairly contentious, there is an argument to be said for separating this team from HR. There is a growing mistrust of HR, as discussed earlier, and the organisation-community has to feel like it is acting on behalf of the employees, rather than the legal interests of the organisation. A community is fluid and evolves organically to the needs of the employees, whereas, in the large part, HR is driven by processes, bureaucracy and law. While there clearly has to be a relationship between the two, the belonging and community team should be independent of HR, ideally reporting straight to the CEO or head of the organisation.

Examples of supportive actions for each characteristic

Characteristic	What works
1 The organisation-community provides according to everybody's individual needs and what they need to thrive and grow	Consider including dedicated resource or even an organisation-community function charged with ensuring all employees are supported to be the best they can be and bring their whole self to work
	System-wide education to understand the specific needs and preferences of minority groups
	Onboarding processes where all new starters are able to communicate individual working preferences
2 The organisation-community protects the well-being and welfare of all employees	Holistic well-being and wellness programme which supports the whole individual – both at work and in their personal lives
	Access to support that is completely confidential and independent of HR
3 Behaviours and values reflect those of wider society norms and the organisation-community provides the psychological safety for all employees to speak up and address intolerable behaviours	Reassess values and behaviour frameworks – are they really delivering value, contributing to a sense of belonging, supporting well-being or leveraging performance?
	Consider developing an organisation-community contract that makes it clear that belonging is a core value of the organisation. Make it clear that there is zero tolerance for anything that compromises this, giving employees the confidence to call out intolerable behaviours
4 The organisation-community's primary concern is providing an environment where every employee is included, supported, accepted and valued	Bring D&I and well-being initiatives together under the organisation-community banner, where belonging is looked at holistically, measured continuously and drives the engagement and performance of all employees

What are you doing now that works and what would you like to change?

Consider which activities you are investing in now, which are supporting the four critical characteristics of the organisation-community and what else you could do.

Characteristic	What is working?	What else could we do?
1 The organisation-community provides according to everybody's individual needs and what they need to thrive and grow		
2 The organisation-community protects the well-being and welfare of all employees		
3 Behaviours and values reflect those of wider society norms and the organisation-community provides the psychological safety for all employees to speak up and address intolerable behaviours		
4 The organisation-community's primary concern is providing an environment where every employee is included, supported, accepted and valued		

Brandwatch: building the organisation-community

Abadesi Osunsade is the VP of Global Community & Belonging, a role that was created by the Brandwatch D&I committee when it was decided that taking a community approach would help to develop shared purpose across cultural boundaries in a world where virtual connectivity is increasingly becoming the norm.

Tech is an area that, to date, has struggled to create diverse workforces and one of the challenges Abadesi is tasked with is exploring where both culture and process are preventing this in Brandwatch. In addition, she is developing external community partnerships that will help to develop the internal community. Although still early days in her role, she is already making great strides and, when I spoke to her, I asked her to name the one thing that she feels is enabling her to progress in her mission. Her answer:

'Genuine commitment and trust from the top – which empowers me to move forward.'

Principle two: Belonging culture – 'Everyone included, everybody thrives'

Characteristic	What works
1 Consistency & transparency	Set communication- and information-sharing standards. Consider the tone, the media, the frequency and consistency of messaging
	Ask the wider organisation about the communications they would like, how and when
	Create resources and platforms to facilitate formal and informal dialogue across the organisation. Consider technology platforms, social media, chat apps, town-hall meetings and daily bulletins
	Communications activity and progress should be reported regularly to the executive team and the wider organisation
2 Connectivity	Create and welcome ideas from employees for organisation initiatives that will increase connectivity between teams
	Ask the employees what charity and social purposes initiatives they would like to support and how
	Create a platform for sharing individual stories that increase understanding of minority groups and other work going on across the wider organisation
	Create opportunities for virtual cross-organisation networking
3 Integrity	Define behavioural standards – not behaviour frameworks
	Frequently communicate what is acceptable and what is unacceptable
	Create a zero-tolerance policy to deal swiftly with proscribed behaviours

What are you doing now that works and what would you like to change?

Consider which activities you are investing in now that are supporting the three attributes of belonging cultures and what else you could do.

Characteristic	What is working?	What else could we do?
1 Consistency & transparency		
2 Connectivity		
3 Integrity		

Principle three: Empowered people – 'My castle'

How others support it

Within organisations and teams, psychological safety is critical for a sense of agency – we need to feel that we are both trusted and can predict the consequences of choices we make.

- Leaders and colleagues can support this by advising and offering insight to the decisions an individual has to make but, ultimately, leave the individual in control of how they move forward.
- Failure should not be admonished or lead to serious consequences, if these were not previously articulated. Psychological safety is damaged when we feel our security is threatened.
- We can help others when they have failed by not apportioning blame, but by helping them to understand what went wrong and what they could do differently next time

How others damage it

There are many ways our sense of agency can be damaged by the structures, processes and behaviours in organisations:

- Where there is strict hierarchy with corresponding power structures, people may feel they are able to exert excessive control over others. The concept of 'excessive control' does indeed vary from culture to culture, but, in this context, I mean where it is above and beyond what is deemed acceptable in that particular culture.
- Processes that knowingly or unknowingly exclude others will take away a sense of agency, which is particularly true of marginalised groups. We cannot feel a sense of agency when we are excluded because this damages both our self-esteem and trust in our own judgement – both of which take away our feeling of being in control of our own actions.
- While structures and processes are tangible and reasonably easy to assess, the behaviour of others is the one most likely to damage our sense of agency, yet is usually the most difficult to detect. Micro-aggressions, 'banter', aggression, bullying, and intentional or unintentional exclusion can make people feel inferior or unworthy. In these situations, intentionally or unintentionally, one person is trying to exert control over another – and, in a social group, this will often lead to a weak sense of agency and, if sustained for a long period, anxiety, stress or depression. For this reason, in belonging cultures, there has to be explicit zero tolerance for these behaviours.

Examples could include:

- *Structure example*
  Hierarchy can be problematic because the very notion of power and striving for the next level creates behaviours and actions that are incongruent with empowerment. Let's take an organisation where there are excessive layers of hierarchy – say, where there are directors and senior directors or marketing managers and senior marketing managers (titles created normally to pacify those who, understanding the nature and importance of hierarchy in the organisation, feel they are not making fast enough progress in their careers). If one of these directors or marketing managers is ear-marked for a promotion to the senior title, two things are likely to happen. First, to ensure they deliver the results they need, they may start to micro-manage, essentially eliminating any empowerment. Second, in an attempt to demonstrate leadership behaviours above their current position (and, more than likely, feeling in competition with others at their level), they may start to take an autocratic approach, asserting excessive power over others – basically, trying to increase their own agency in a situation where they feel they have little control. Hierarchy in organisations can often be the enemy of creating a sense of agency in employees.

- *Process example*

  Many processes in organisations unwittingly have negative effects on employees. Let's take the example of a typical recruitment process, such as:

  - Receive application with CV and covering letter via web application.

  - Complete online psychometrics interview.

  - Attend an assessment centre, including multiple interviews and exercises.

  Each stage is designed to give you an insight into the applicant, but also has the potential to take a sense of agency from some applicants.

  - *Receive application with CV and covering letter via web application* – why is the cover letter important in the process unless you are hiring somebody who has to write copy? This takes agency from those who may be dyslexic as well as many others for whom this is not a strength.

  - *Complete online psychometrics interview* – I have a real problem with the use of psychometrics in recruitment processes. If there are specific capabilities required for a role that you can assess through psychometrics, then this may be acceptable. But the use of personality psychometrics? Is it ever acceptable to make a judgement on somebody's personality? Many will argue that there is no right or wrong in personality assessments but I argue the contrary. One well-known psychometric has two specific categories that measure neuroticism and conscientiousness. I don't know about you, but I have never come across a role that specifically asks for candidates with high neuroticism and low conscientiousness. Another consideration here is that the use of psychometrics could discriminate against neurodivergent candidates, given that some of the traits measured may be a result of their condition.

  - *Attend an assessment centre, including multiple interviews and exercises* – assessment centres really need a rethink. First, they create no sense of agency for those who are introverts, are neurodivergent or who have other disabilities and there is yet to be definitive evidence that assessment centres predict job performance. In addition, the aspects of public-speaking that are deemed 'good' are more often affiliated with men rather than women (Mary Beard's book *Women and Power* is an excellent book on the origins and remaining impact of this), thereby creating advantage for that group.

  Processes in organisations should be closely examined to see where they disadvantage others, and redesigned in a way that enables the talents of everybody to be showcased and leveraged.

- *Behaviour example*

  In an attempt to drive the right behaviours and culture, many organisations will use behaviour frameworks, normally related to the organisational values, as a measure included in performance reviews. However, for the large part, they are unsuccessful in impacting the lived experience of employees. Take, for example, passive aggressive behaviours – those where the intent is to exert power over someone else, but done in a way that can seem acceptable – if not exemplary – within a behaviour framework. A leader who is working with a larger group to identify people for a critical project dismisses the suggestion of somebody with significant experience and knowledge required for the project, put forward by another member of the group. The reason given is that this person lacks the resilience to get involved in such a critical, complex project and that it would probably be unfair to set them up to fail. The others around the leader may not know said employee personally so, take the leaders word. Not just that, but, rather than just impacting the employee's involvement in this project, potentially their ongoing career may suffer, as an imposed impression from the leader may change the employee's reputation with others. This is exclusion (and taking away control) at its very best – and, unfortunately, most common.

As proposed in the actions for developing the organisation-community, behaviour frameworks are, perhaps, not the answer – genuinely committing to a speak-up and zero-tolerance culture almost certainly will.

How curiosity can be encouraged

If you want employees to be curious about others in your organisation, there must be the psychological safety to allow them to do so. This comes mainly from organisational initiatives to open up the conversations, such as those that provide a platform for diverse voices, and for leaders to role model 'curiosity' behaviours.

How curiosity can be damaged

General curiosity can be stifled by a bureaucratic, risk-averse environment and, if there is an over-emphasis on the legal implications of discrimination, it creates a culture of fear where employees are unlikely to act in any way that they feel may impact their job security. In addition, and, ironically, there are some D&I initiatives that can actually prevent curiosity between individuals and groups. There is evidence to suggest that certain approaches to unconscious bias or inclusivity can, in fact, be divisive if they inadvertently highlight the differences between people or suggest that one group has a bias towards another (often inciting fear that the biases may be interpreted as discrimination, engendering subsequent defensive behaviours).

- *Structure example*
  Curiosity will be stifled in an organisation where there are siloed functions and teams. These silos emerge inadvertently to protect resources and to create safety

in 'blame-cultures', effectively building a wall between the team and the rest of the organisation. This creates an obstacle to employees within and outside each team, essentially indicating that curiosity is not encouraged by the organisation. These obstacles also exist where there is strict hierarchy and power walls are built between leaders and the rest of the organisation. The message 'You are allowed to be curious, but not here' simply won't cut it in a belonging culture.

- *Process example*
  Bureaucracy really is the enemy of curiosity. When the COVID crisis hit and organisations were forced to close offices, employees, united by the common goal of maintaining business continuity, rolled up their sleeves and set about creating new working practices. Non-essential bureaucracy and restrictive procedures were disregarded and organisations started to see the innovation and agility they had been striving towards for years emerge within days. Employee and cross-team collaborations were greater than ever and informal teams and connections were made in response to the urgent need for solutions. When no one knows the answer, curiosity is the only way. Organisations can encourage this behaviour by creating an environment where people constantly ask, 'What if there is a better solution than this?'

- *Behaviour example*
  Leaders and line managers have the greatest responsibility when it comes to fostering curiosity. Leadership style has a make-or-break impact on how curious individuals are within a team. Micro-management, controlling behaviours, process-driven approaches, risk-aversion and lack of curiosity will dampen any motivation team members have to be curious. In addition, line managers who have more frequent interactions and overtly stronger relationships with some team members will stifle the desire for team members to get to know one another – in this case the leader's lack of curiosity about everyone in the team results in poor team cohesion and collaboration.

How open-mindedness can be encouraged

The organisational culture, processes and leadership behaviours should all be aligned on encouraging open-mindedness. The organisation can increase understanding of those in marginalised groups by giving them a voice to share stories and ensure physical symbols that demonstrate open-mindedness are included across the organisation. This could include, for example:

- diverse representation in marketing materials
- diverse representation in internal display materials

- ensuring things such as magazines or reading materials in waiting areas are not directed to one particular audience
- meeting room names that reflect diversity
- being aware of having pictures of previous organisation leaders on display if these are representative of a narrow prototype
- providing a diverse range of foods suitable for all dietary requirements, cultures and preferences.

Organisations should provide education for all on differences and minority groups to create empathy and acceptance, and leaders should role model open-minded behaviours in all their activities.

How open-mindedness can be damaged

The biggest risk to open-mindedness is a culture that is not progressive and where leadership is clearly not open-minded – where some minority groups seem a more palatable group for which to promote understanding than others and where decision making is confined to homogenous leadership teams. Fear in blame cultures can cause people to close in rather than reach out, which stifles the motivation to seek out the perspectives of others, causing an emotional disconnect between employees and the organisation.

- *Structure example*
  Fixed homogenous teams tend to create group-think, which prevents both innovation and open-mindedness. The sorts of teams that seem to reflect this and spend less time in activities where they will collaborate with a diverse range of employees tend to be at the top of the organisation, particularly in those organisations where senior leaders value the power of hierarchy. I have had experiences of working with such senior leadership teams, who are often frustrated and perplexed at the lack of ownership and innovative thinking in the organisation – entirely unaware of the fact that they are the most significant blocker to these behaviours.

- *Process example*
  Command and control decision-making processes, with guidelines enforcing a strict decision sign-off hierarchy, prevent the contribution, and voice, of others to decisions that guide the progress of the organisation. This type of archaic bureaucracy should be applicable to decisions regarding compliance, regulation and legislation. In an organisation-community, to ensure everyone feels a sense of belonging and emotional connection to a common purpose, unnecessary bureaucracy should be minimised.

- *Behaviour example*
  A situation that I come across frequently is where one particular type of leadership personality is significantly over-represented, signalling that the organisation values particular personalities over others. In many industries, this is a systemic issue where often extrovert and forceful personalities tend to progress more than others. In turn, this means that those who are not like this are not given a voice and fail to progress because these leaders judge the behaviours of their team members by those of their own, which they have been led to believe have contributed to their success.

Examples of supportive actions for each attribute

Characteristic	What works
1 Agency	Before new employees join the organisation, encourage line managers to have early-stage conversations designed to develop in-depth understanding of each individual and their circumstances
	Ensure onboarding and induction procedures reflect the value of identity and the importance of agency
	Ensure the organisation-community team can provide training, support and resources on resilience and confidence
	Provide allyship training and resources, encouraging allies to provide support and speak up on behalf of those who may be marginalised
	Assess the organisational structure. Are there unnecessary layers of management? If there are, be bold and propose flattening the organisation. Acknowledge and address where there appear to be toxic bubbles of power, making structure, role and people changes as required. If you really want this culture to evolve some drastic moves may be needed
	Conduct an in-depth process audit to identify and remove all the overt and subtle aspects that exclude some employees and damage their sense of agency
2 Curiosity	Train managers to have 'brave conversations'
	Use storytelling to increase understanding and open up conversations. Set up virtual or physical 'Curiosity Camps' – think TED Talks – for organisations where people are invited to submit and share their stories
	Set up a reverse mentoring scheme where leaders are mentored by employees from minority or marginalised groups

Characteristic	What works
3 Open-mindedness	Provide resources and training on judgement and bias. Rather than focusing on individual unconscious biases, increase understanding of why we make implicit associations and how to break them
	Make a concerted effort to create leadership teams that are diverse in personality, style and identity. Bring high-potential employees into leadership team processes, meetings and decision making to ensure the contribution of diverse perspectives
	Provide a variety of ways for people to share their voice, opinions and ideas, to support more introverted employees. Don't provide training in an effort to make them more confident about speaking up and challenging in the moment – it is not the individuals who need changing, it is the environment in which they operate that should adapt

What are you doing now that works and what would you like to change?

Consider which activities you are investing in now that are supporting the three attributes of empowered individuals and what else you could do.

Characteristic	What is working?	What else could we do?
1 Agency		
2 Curiosity		
3 Open-mindedness		

Principle four: Identity-centred leadership – 'Leaders as facilitators'

The identity-centred leader as the facilitator of talent

The role of the leader in this respect is to connect with each individual as a unique identity and to tune into their needs, motivations and aspirations. As I have said many times, this is not a one-size-fits-all approach to leadership – this is a one-size-fits-one. This requires a very different approach to leadership development as the focus is not on managing performance, delegation, motivation or any other traditional development themes. There is a shift from management being done to the individuals in a uniform, consistent way, to the manager serving the needs of each unique identity.

The leader has to develop an understanding of 'equity' rather than 'equality' in the team members – making them aware that equality comes from the fact that everybody gets what they need to ensure they can maximise their individual talents.

The identity-centred leader as the facilitator of connectivity

As a driver of connectivity, the leader has to focus on creating positive energy in the team by:

- *Connecting to individuals:* finding a unique connection to each individual such that deep mutual trust develops. This trust is the foundation of psychological safety.
- *Connecting individuals in teams:* this doesn't mean that the leader must facilitate the relationship between each person in the team, but create shared standards, goals, beliefs and practices, creating a common interest around which individuals are able to connect. This may sound like any traditional leadership role, but the critical thing here is that the leader connects to the individual first, creating the psychological safety for all team members to organically connect. The leader should role model, creating a sense of belonging when someone new joins the team, by spending time getting to know more about the individual and making a more personal introduction to the team. Strong connectivity in this context supports team agility, innovation, performance and well-being.

- *Connecting individuals and teams to the organisation:* the identity-centred leader drives individual emotional connectivity and team connectivity with the organisation by creating the psychological safety for individuals to be curious about the wider organisation. This can be facilitated by the leader being a communication bridge and by leaders working together to create opportunities for teams to get to know one another, collaborate and learn from each other. This is particularly critical when considering leadership in virtual working.
- *Connecting the organisation to the team:* organisation-communities foster a sense of belonging by consistently demonstrating open-mindedness in communications, decision making, strategy development and all other activities. This doesn't mean making a democratic process of everything, but the responsibility of the leader is to connect the organisation to the team so that there is recognition of the talents, innovations, working practices and activities that could contribute to wider organisational practice or performance. This connectivity can be formalised by regular leadership comms to the executive team, but is far more effective if it is done through self-driven, informal approaches. Whether this will work depends on where your organisation currently is on the organisation-community scale.

The identity-centred leader as the facilitator of well-being and wellness

As I have said, the identity-centred leader is a critical link in connecting team members to the organisation-community and fostering a sense of belonging. One of their core responsibilities in this sense is facilitating the well-being and wellness of all their direct reports. This requires leaders to develop an understanding of the behavioural norms of their team members and develop a 'barometer' that recognises small shifts in each individual that might indicate changes in well-being or wellness. In conjunction with developing trust so that team members feel able to communicate when they need additional support, the leadership barometer allows leaders to leverage the sense of belonging by anticipating the needs of each employee.

Teams led by leaders who have a curious mindset and encourage the same in others tend to be motivated, energised and feel a binding sense of purpose. Teams like this are an unstoppable force. They constantly ask 'Why?' or 'How can we do this better?' They never give up, but they are more than happy to change direction. They aren't afraid to say 'I don't know', but they will always put energy behind finding out. They challenge outside and inside the team, engaging in healthy conflict within problem solving, which serves to deepen the connections between team members. They move forward with purpose. They over-achieve. They innovate. They have fun. And they all behave like individual human beings, not employees conforming to a prescribed set of behaviours.

Examples of supportive actions for each attribute

Characteristic	What works
1 Curiosity	Introduce design-thinking workshops to encourage leaders to approach problem solving differently
	Devolve as much decision-making power as possible to team leaders. Outside of regulatory and legal requirements, consider which other decisions genuinely require central control. Clarity around accountability is critical, but people are more likely to feel accountable for things over which they have made the decisions
	Assess and rethink leadership programmes. On what are you basing their ROI? What type of development or support do your leaders need to become identity-focused leaders?
2 Courage	Provide coaches to support leaders in finding their voice and keeping their values front of mind in all activities
	Encourage calculated risks by sharing successes where it has paid off and ensuring processes do not encourage risk aversion or covering up of mistakes
	Executive teams to agree and share their team standards in terms of acknowledging and addressing proscribed behaviours to demonstrate that they too are willing to be held to account
3 Humanity	Strip out corporate speak from communications, marketing materials, meetings, training, *everything*!
	Provide development support and team development for the executive team to develop and role model the skill of leading with humanity
	Assess which processes and policies don't put people first and have the potential to inadvertently cause suffering or disadvantage to some employees, for example parental leave, maternity or bereavement policies that do not acknowledge and, therefore, exclude individual circumstances such as IVF, miscarriage, still birth, adoption or fostering

What are you doing now that works and what would you like to change?

Consider which activities you are investing in now that are supporting the desired attributes of identity-centred leaders and what else you could do.

Characteristic	What is working?	What else could we do?
1 Curiosity		
2 Courage		
3 Humanity		

Principle five: Connected teams – 'Our castle'

Connected teams are the sum of the previous principles and, therefore, in essence, can emerge only if the other elements are embedded – that is, a sense of community, a belonging culture, empowered individuals and leaders as facilitators enable the characteristics of connected teams to develop. They are, therefore, pre-requisites for connected teams.

Examples of supportive actions for each attribute

Characteristic	What works
1 Dynamism	Provide problem-solving and design-thinking workshops for teams
	Encourage teams to define, reach out and pitch to the organisation for resources or requests related to transformation according to internal and external needs, being accountable for the return on investment
2 Self-direction	Provide access to ongoing team development support rather than doing a one-off workshop or providing team development training exclusively to managers
	Encourage team leaders to help teams define how they will collectively make decisions
3 Collective conscious	Reassess performance metrics reward systems. What opportunities are there to change the focus from individual to collective performance? What opportunities are there for shared equity?
	Allow teams to define, measure, monitor and continually evolve their own internal metrics, goals and objectives

What are you doing now that works and what would you like to change?

Consider which activities you are investing in now that are supporting the three attributes of connected teams and what else you could do.

Characteristic	What is working?	What else could we do?
1 Dynamism		
2 Self-direction		
3 Collective conscious		

Targets and KPIs: what gets measured, gets done (often badly)

I have always cringed at this trite, management-speak phrase, which reduces the success of every activity in organisations down to a set of numbers that most of the time have become largely disconnected from the object of the exercise. At this point, most strategic planning guidance would point you to start looking for external benchmarks for D&I, but I am going to swim against the tide on this.

Do not use external benchmarks.

No matter how well-researched they may profess to be, every set of D&I benchmarks I have ever come across – even those that are widely used and present global benchmarks – are still clinging on to the old what gets measured gets done adage. The benchmarks are still number-led, activity-led and use public sharing of targets and progress as the zenith of D&I excellence. I saw an article recently that ranked the top 10 most inclusive organisations according to the following criteria:

- gender pay gap data
- D&I programmes
- internal LGBT+ and BAME networks
- gender divide on boards
- disability awareness policies
- D&I media coverage.

What do any of these activities tell you about the actual experience of employees in the organisation? Nothing whatsoever. As we have seen, tribunals are averted, trouble-makers are exited and silenced with NDAs, while prioritisation of financial results means poor behaviour with drive exclusion often going unchecked. The performance indicators above provide no insight into any of these incidents. This is hindering the development of inclusion not just in organisations, but in society as a whole. It is morally wrong. Executive teams, management boards and shareholders must develop a moral conscience, take responsibility and turn the tide in organisations.

Finally, bring it all together

For each of the risks and opportunities identified in the Belonging Audit in Chapter 3, and the activities you have identified using this chapter, your plan will include:

- the vision
- each of the articulated themes

- high-level actions and timelines
- who will be the owner of each of the actions
- how you will measure progress for each theme. Include:
  - the percentage targets, such as improvements in Belonging Audit scores for particular employee groups or representation of minority groups in particular areas of the business *and*
  - the employee experience targets that add a dose of reality to the data and give progress credibility
- what you hope to achieve in years 1, 3 and 5 for each of the themes.

The template below shows how to format your plan. The content under 'Theme 1' should be repeated for each of your identified themes.

The vision:

Theme 1:

The how

Organisational structure

Actions	Key steps & dates	Ownership

Procedures, process, policy

Actions	Key steps & dates	Ownership

Leadership development

Actions	Key steps & dates	Ownership

Education & training

Actions	Key steps & dates	Ownership

Support & resources

Actions	Key steps & dates	Ownership

Recruitment career progression & retention

Action	Key steps & dates	Ownership

How we will measure progress

Data metrics	*Employee experience*

What we will achieve

Year 1	
Year 3	
Year 5	

chapter 5

Get buy-in from the organisation

You might be forgiven for thinking the hard work is done now that you have collected the data and created your plan, but the trickiest part is yet to come. A great deal of thought and effort must go into thinking about how to create a business case and pitch the plan you have put together in a way that will resonate with, and gain commitment from, the decision makers. To support this, this chapter will look at:

- how to design the value proposition in a way that will get approval from the decision makers

- using narrative and data to ensure decision makers feel compelled to act and are emotionally committed to moving forward

- deciding the critical success factors of the plan that need commitment from the executive or senior team

- building advocates to create wider engagement and ensure maximum value and implementation

Build a robust business case that appeals directly to your audience

Before you begin developing the business case, be clear about what you are asking of them, who your audience is, and how they are most likely to be influenced.

What are you asking of your audience?

First, define exactly what it is you are asking of them. Consider the following:

- Are you asking for full-scale commitment to the plan or are you asking to get started on a smaller scale, by doing a pilot, for example?
- Are you asking for budget equal to or above current D&I spend?
- Is there an existing, embedded D&I plan you are asking to replace with this plan or will this be the first time such a plan is implemented?
- Are you asking for commitment to actions that have broader implications for the organisation? For example, if you are asking for a new function to be created or even new roles, what are the implications for the wider business?

What do you know about your audience?

With the 'asks' in mind, building a detailed picture of the intended audience will help you to build a narrative and pitch the plan in a way that will engage and drive commitment from the decision makers. Thinking about this will not only help you to create a compelling pitch, but will also mean you can consider a range of scenarios or objections ahead of presenting and have in mind how to handle them to prevent the pitch from going off course.

Question	Considerations	Your thoughts
Who will be there?	List the decision makers who will be present when you make your pitch	
Who do you know?	Which of these decision makers are you familiar with and what do you know about them? For those you are not familiar with, list who you can ask for insights that will help you to plan the pitch	
Is there D&I interest in the group?	Who, if anyone, in the group has a particular interest in D&I? How can you engage them prior to the pitch?	

Question	Considerations	Your thoughts
How will decisions be made?	Is there one key decision maker in the group or will commitment depend on consensus? If there is one key decision maker, list what will be their key priorities. If the decision will depend on consensus, who may prove to be the most difficult? How can you mitigate the risk prior to the pitch? What will appeal to them specifically during the pitch?	
Who has the greatest influence in the group?	Is there a strong influencer in the group who others tend to follow in opinion? How can you engage them prior to and during the pitch?	
Who are your allies?	Are there one or more key members of the group you would consider advocates? Can you engage them before presenting the business case to the wider group to gain their support in the pitch?	
What are the current business priorities?	Are there any current pressing business issues that might mean your plan might not get as much support as it could or mean it is not seen as a priority? If so, who can you speak to now to see if this is the right time to pitch or if it should wait?	
What is the group decision-making style?	Is the group apt to long deliberation and a preference to see all the detail? Or do they prefer fast pace, punchy messages and clear calls to action? What does this mean for how you pitch and the materials you provide? With this in mind, who in your team would be best to lead on the pitch?	
Are the group trailblazers or risk-adverse?	Do the team like to be pioneers or do they prefer to rely on experience? If they like to be pioneers, how can you weave this message into the pitch, for example drawing on what competitors are doing in this area? If they prefer to rely on experience, what evidence and expertise in the area of belonging can you include in your pitch? Consider including data from consultancy research regarding belonging or refer to organisations who are already focusing on this as a priority	

▶

Question	Considerations	Your thoughts
What are the potential objections?	What other objections might there be? Who can you share the pitch with who will not be at the meeting but may be able to give you more insights into what objections there may be?	
How diverse is the group?	What implications does this have when preparing and presenting the pitch? What might this mean in terms of how you might adjust the key messages?	

Creating this document up front makes a significant difference in your likelihood of success. Whether you like it or not, when you are pitching an idea, you are, essentially, a salesperson and all successful salespeople will tell you that knowing your customer is the number-one priority. As you go through the process of building the business case and preparing the pitch, keep checking back to this document and ensure you are creating a proposition that appeals uniquely to your audience.

Now, create your value proposition

A compelling value proposition has to feel personal, be directly relevant to your organisation and appeal to the intended audience. Your value proposition should speak to the themes described in the plan and, although the Belonging Plan itself shouldn't be built around current business objectives, in this context, it should be aligned to other business priorities to support commitment from the decision makers.

- First, consider some of the current strategic business priorities in the organisation.
- Then, consider which of these priorities are 'gains' – opportunities for growth – and which are 'pains' – problems that need to be solved or risks to be mitigated.
- Then, consider the belonging themes around which your plan is built and where there is the opportunity to add value towards the business priorities.
- Don't try to shoe-horn in all the business priorities (I have seen this done more times in my career than I would like). Just one or two strong value creators can be very impactful.

Examples

Strategic priorities		Belonging themes	
Gains	Pains	Opportunity for gain	Pain relief
Fostering innovation to increase market share	Attracting and retaining top talent in a difficult talent market	Increasing representation of marginalised groups will create a more diverse workforce, which has been proven to increase innovation	Actively engaging with and attracting a broader range of candidates will tap into more diverse talent, and a focus on ensuring everyone feels that they belong will increase retention
Developing new products to break into an emerging market	Increasing resiliency and agility for business continuity in a volatile environment	Focusing on attracting diverse talent brings diversity of thought, skills and experience to support innovative product development	A sense of belonging increases engagement and creates psychological safety, which has been proven to be central to agile organisations

Bringing these priorities and themes together will create your value proposition statement. So, for example, if the business priorities you had identified were:

- improve brand perception to attract more female talent, which is significantly under-represented compared to competitors
- foster innovation to increase market share
- the need to protect mental health and well-being during a volatile, uncertain period

and you had identified the following themes:

- under-representation of women in technology teams
- a significant drop in diversity after first line management
- a poor sense of belonging and increased absence rates in some areas of the business

then, your value proposition might be:

> 'The Belonging Plan will take an holistic approach to diversity, inclusion and well-being by making sure everyone feels that they belong to our organisation. In doing so, we will be able to address the gender balance in the tech teams, which is a particular challenge of our industry, by focusing on attracting talent from different communities and increasing retention by supporting career progress. In addition, by creating a culture of belonging, which research has shown supports well-being, increases performance and drives innovation, we can enable greater diversity in the leadership population and improve engagement across the whole organisation.'

Have a go at identifying and aligning your plan to some of your organisation's strategic priorities. Then create a narrative for the value proposition:

Strategic priorities		Belonging themes	
Gains	Pains	Opportunity for gain	Pain relief
Value proposition			

Create a pitch presentation with a hard-hitting narrative

Visualise the audience in situ

If you have presented to this group before, close your eyes and visualise the room.

- How did they greet you or you greet them when you came into the room?
- What were their facial expressions and body language like when you were presenting?
- Were their facial expressions and body language different when you left the room?

When you present the belonging business case and plan, it has to *feel* different from the moment you walk into the room to the moment you leave. If you are presenting at a monthly management board meeting, the agenda is usually tightly packed and various presenters are rolled in and out like a production line, pitching their requests while the team members become increasingly bored and frustrated at not being able to get what they consider the real priorities on the agenda. If you can't persuade the team to receive your presentation outside of the monthly meeting, then you need to make a concerted effort to make your pitch different and make each member of the team want to sit up and listen. Lead the presentation with the passion and belief that you have in this as an issue the organisation cannot afford to ignore.

Think about the following:

- What you want them to think and feel about the pitch – at the start, in the middle and when you leave the room. Engagement and commitment are outputs of an emotional response. What should that response be? Anger? Shame? Sadness? Excitement? Relief? This should help you to create the right narrative.
- What type of information will appeal to the various members of the team? How will you intertwine data and narrative so that the essence of neither is lost?
- What body language and facial expressions will indicate the emotional reaction you want to create? How will you recognise engagement, buy-in and the desire to commit to moving forward?

Structure a narrative to appeal to hearts and minds

We have looked previously at how belonging cultures bring the humanity back into organisations and use stories to increase understanding between people. Using these principles when you create and deliver your narrative will be key to making the presentation of your proposed plan *feel* different. Bringing the human element in, backed up with hard data and facts, gives you the greatest opportunity to develop cognitive and emotional commitment to the cause. And it is the emotional commitment that endures and compels people to act.

Stories traditionally follow a predictable pattern driven by the variables of tension and time. Using this pattern, you can engage both hearts and minds, ensuring the outcome is a genuine commitment to action. The data analysis leads to insights that create the narrative, but, as I said, the data itself should not lead the narrative – it should be used to give high-level results or to amplify a particular point. The structure of your presentation can be built around this pattern known as the narrative arc (Figure 5.1).

The narrative arc framework allows you to:

- build intrigue and tension from minute one by describing the process and what insights you were looking for
- present the high-level data analyses, results in figures, and include where the results are both positive and negative

Figure 5.1 The narrative arc

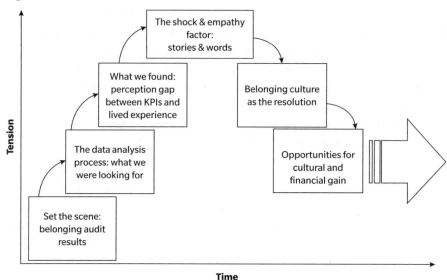

- create a 'climax' of the narrative, where tension should be highest and, in this case, is in the form of the shock and empathy factor
- decrease the tension when the belonging culture is proposed as an investment to resolve the current situation with the potential for financial gain. Here you will include stories from those who say that they do feel a sense of belonging to build a picture of the belonging culture you propose to build
- conclude the narrative with tension higher at the end of the presentation, with the audience feeling compelled to act
- leave the audience feeling a sense of 'not on my watch'.

Set the scene

The impact you make here determines the level of engagement for the rest of your pitch. It is your opportunity to not only show that this is different from the typical D&I approaches in the past, but also to fend off some of the doubts that may be presented early by the sceptics or those who have D&I fatigue. This is where you start building intrigue. For example:

> 'We feel that the traditional approach to D&I doesn't tell us much about how individual employees experience the organisation. We wanted to know how many of our employees feel that they *belong* in our organisation, so we decided to find out . . . '

The data analysis process

Describe how you executed the research, but keep it simple. The main point here is to show that the process was robust and so, the results are significant. Explaining the essence of the survey and the other data sources you used in the analysis will further add to the intrigue, building anticipation about what the analysis found.

What we found: create compelling stories with your data

I can't tell you the number of times in my career I have sat through presentations that deliver slide after slide of data, driven largely by the presenter's need to showcase the pain-staking number-crunching and analysis they have done to get to a mediocre conclusion. I have always loved the moment when they get to the end of their 152 slides and ask, 'Any questions?' to a room full of people who have been jolted awake by the punctuating question.

Please stop doing this! Stop eating up valuable working hours with nonsense. For the one person in the room who wants the detail, send them a report. For everyone else, give them a reason to listen. When pitching your plan, you want to weave your data into narratives that lead the audience towards an emotional response. Make sure you know your data and have it to hand for any awkward questions, but, in presenting, use the data to drive to a narrative conclusion.

Present an overview of the high-level results, presenting the hotspots and coldspots identified in the analysis. But, for the main part, you are looking to build compelling narratives around each one of your identified themes, such as:

'Neurodivergent employees who have disclosed their conditions represent 8% of our 5,000 employees, with an average salary of £30,000. This is a group we have targeted in recruitment as it is reported that between 15% and 20% of the population have a neurodivergent condition. In addition, a great deal of research points to the innovation value this population can bring due to their different thinking and specialist talents. However, this group of employees was one of the top groups who reported not feeling a sense of belonging in the organisation. They also represent one of the employee groups with the higher rates of absence – an average of 20 days per year, costing us £1.8 million in lost productivity alone. Research shows that 85% of absence in this group is due to mental health issues related to stress in the workplace. Not only are we losing out on the potential value this talent could bring, but it would also appear that we are failing to protect their health and well-being.'

Keep your slides simple, so that the focus is on the narrative not the screen. Use visuals to make an impact. For example, the key fact in the narrative above is the £1.8 million – having this number on a slide with nothing else will add to the impact.

The shock and empathy factor

'For sale: baby shoes. Never worn.'

Unknown author

Using only six words, the example above demonstrates the significant power stories have in evoking universal emotional reactions. Human beings have in-depth understanding of shared emotions that can be unwilfully summoned by a narrative – in this example, we all know what loss feels like and the poignancy of losing a child is evoked by these words. Belonging is a universal emotional need that we pursue our whole lives so, like loss, we all know what the pain of rejection and exclusion feels like. Your narrative has to include stories that emotionally transport the audience to these feelings, the experience of which evokes a sense of responsibility and need to act. While the data and facts are important, as is the financial incentivisation to commit to the plan, it is this experience that will create enduring emotional commitment.

I truly believe that this emotional connectivity to the human experience of exclusion is what will make the difference to how leaders and teams across all types of organisations will start to think about belonging. This is where you start to share the experiences shared by those in the organisation who feel the least sense of belonging – this is where you give the data a human voice. Be creative about how you present it. Pat Wadors, former chief talent officer at ServiceNow, tells the story of a friend who surveyed his organisation to understand how the employees experienced belonging. He took some of the experiences shared by employees who did not feel a sense of belonging in the organisation and had voice-over actors recount their stories. When presenting his plan to the leadership team, at this point in the pitch, he had the lights lowered and played the recordings to the room. When the lights came up, about half of the leaders were crying.

Another way is to tell a 'reverse story', which helps the audience to 'walk in someone else's shoes'. Give the voice a face by telling the story as though it had happened to someone else, somewhere else. Say it is your partner, or sister, or son. Put a photograph on a slide. People understand these relationships and therefore find it easier to empathise, or imagine if it was happening to someone in their life. In addition, if you and the audience are not from a minority group, the story may seem to be more shocking. Then you remove the photo and tell them that this did not happen to someone in your life, but to someone within the organisation. The power of the emotional reaction they had previously can have a huge impact on changing perspectives.

Belonging culture as the resolution and then present the value proposition

This is where you demonstrate why a focus on belonging is the answer and how it is different from traditional D&I. Again, keep it simple. Use the belonging at work description, the principles or the underlying values as described in Part 1. This part should be brief and serve as a link to the value proposition, which has more direct relevance to the audience.

Share the plan and ask for commitment

This is the most risky part. The focus here has to be on maintaining the emotional commitment you have developed to this point. Present a plan on a page rather than the whole thing, as this can direct the conversation to distracting minutiae, which will dilute the impact you have had so far, as well as subconsciously signal complexity or difficulty. Focus on the asks you identified earlier, and keep referring back to the value proposition when answering questions. If you have done a good job at connecting the audience emotionally so far, and your plan doesn't present any major obstacles, you're almost home and dry.

Critical team commitments

Once you have engaged the team and gained agreement to move forward with the plan, it is important to stress the importance of each team member personally committing to it and being clear on what their specific team commitments are within this:

- The whole team must agree to hold one another accountable for behaving and acting in a way that supports the development of a project plan.
- The team must agree that they are willing to call out and be called out on contrary behaviours in all situations.
- Every individual must commit to developing their leadership approach according to the best practice outline in the plan.
- The team must agree that they are willing to regularly hear your perspective on their performance in this context.

- The team must agree that they will wholeheartedly engage with a plan to develop their leadership approach individually and as a team.
- The leader of the team must agree that there will be zero tolerance and no cover up of contrary behaviours and actions.

So many initiatives in organisations have no substance and create little change because commitment from the top team is not specified clearly enough. Make this initiative different. Show them that you mean business. They do not own the plan, but they are accountable for their role in its success.

Sponsorship, advocacy and stakeholders

Once you have commitment from the decision makers and before you start to implement the plan, think about who you need to engage or manage in order to minimise risks and maximise opportunities.

1 *Identify an influential sponsor*

Identifying an influential sponsor who is passionate about belonging and committed to the plan is fundamental in driving momentum. Ideally, this should be somebody on the executive/decision-making team, who will be able to do things such as negotiate budgets, if required, as well as continuing to belong on the executive agenda. They will be a part of the project decision making as well as a key influencer. Things to consider:

- What level of influence does the sponsor have within the decision-making team?
- What area of the organisation do they lead? If possible, avoid appointing the HR director, who is clearly a stakeholder, but it may mean the plan is pushed into 'another HR project' bracket.
- What else are they currently involved with that may cause conflicting priorities?
- Who in the team is the sort of person that is renowned for getting things done or creating novel solutions? Somebody with energy who can contribute ideas would be ideal.
- If you are a global organisation, consider appointing local sponsors to keep the project on the local agenda.

Once you have agreed and appointed the sponsor, ensure that you contract around their role and how you will work together. All too often, sponsors agree to projects without considering how they will contribute and what the team requires from them.

2 *Map, engage and monitor your stakeholders*

Identifying and managing stakeholders is more about mitigating the risk of the plan being destabilised by those who are typically opposed to D&I projects or those who may become obstructive if they are not consulted, than it is about leveraging the influence of those you know you can engage.

- *Identify:* stakeholders fall into one of two categories – those who will contribute and those who will be impacted. In the context of the Belonging Plan, consider who you will be asking to get involved and do work and those such as leaders who will be responsible for supporting, embedding and communicating the plan within their functions.
- *Prioritise:* use the power-interest model (Figure 5.2) to group your stakeholders according to their interest in and power over the success of the project. This will inform how each group will be managed and where the most collaboration is required.
- *Engage:* create a communication plan for each box of the grid outlining who you will share the plan with, the level of detail or awareness required, when you will share it and how. Think about the relationships people within the team have with each stakeholder and assign according to the levels of trust. Think about how you can leverage the sponsor to engage stakeholders where they have strong relationships.

Figure 5.2 The Power Interest Grid
Source: Developed by Aubrey L. Mendelow

	Low power	High power
High interest	**Subjects** Involve and keep satisfied	**Players** Collaborate and manage closely
Low interest	**Crowd** Monitor and inform	**Context setters** Consult and keep informed

3 *Develop advocacy*

It is worth spending a bit of time thinking about which people, teams or groups around the business will create momentum by telling the belonging story for you. Spend time sharing the plan and ask for ideas and input. Consider:

- *HR and communications:* you will be working hand in hand with them going forward so, energise and engage them early. Ask them to contribute ideas and incorporate suggestions they make.
- *Networks and their sponsors:* what networks exist in the organisation? Be thorough and inclusive when looking at this. It is easy to reach out to the more visible networks such as Women or LGBTQ+, but look for the smaller or less formal groups. For example, I do a lot of work with Neurodivergent Parent networks in large organisations, but this is unlikely to come onto the radar of many employees outside of it. If there are no formal records or processes for such networks or groups in the organisation, it may just be a matter of asking around. Engaging the sponsors of these networks will also be useful for creating greater advocacy at senior levels.
- *Regional teams:* in larger or global organisations, consider who will be your advocates in the regions. Make sure you fully engage both HR and communications teams in the regions just as you would the central teams. This is where projects tend to fail – the sense of community becomes very low where there is too much of a central focus and local leaders don't feel motivated to implement plans over which they have not been fully engaged. Give regions control over adapting and evolving the plan to suit the needs locally.
- *What regional groups or networks are there?* This is an important one, as these will differ between countries. For example, in some countries, there will be indigenous networks while, in others, LGBTQ+ groups may be as visible or be as prevalent.

chapter 6

Put your Belonging Plan into action

So, you have your plan and you have commitment from the leadership team. Now, it is time to start making change happen and, with this in mind, this chapter will help you to:

- understand how implementing the change will differ from traditional programmes
- create a team who will be the 'hub' of the community
- share the plan with the wider organisation
- assess where in the employee lifecycle there are opportunities for processes and practices to embed belonging
- consider and mitigate attitudes that could impact engagement

Not the typical transformation approach

So, this is the part where I am supposed to tell you to create a roadmap or project plan, but I am going to buck the trend again. I truly believe that most culture change programmes fail because they are managed dogmatically by spreadsheet. Culture change is simply about behaviour change (I say simply, but obviously we know behaviour change is anything but simple . . .) and I just don't believe you can create and embed behaviour change this way. Processes, project plans and spreadsheets give people a sense of security – in so far as they are certain about, and can evidence, what they have done and what they are going to do. I am not proposing you throw all caution to the wind and adopt a scattergun approach, of course there has to be a degree of planning and coordination. However, the nature of a community means that it evolves around the people rather than something that is imposed. This may seem an impossible ask, particularly in large organisations, but consider the following:

- *Go where the energy is.* Once you get started, if you find that you get traction in one particular area, focus energy and resource there, then see where it leads to. This is how the community and sense of belonging can develop organically rather than implementing your plan step-by-step, regardless of progress.
- *Keep the conversation going.* Keep the team talking to as many employees as possible to keep getting insights from the ground. Pulse surveys might give you some insights, but chatting is where you uncover the real gems.
- *Local communities within a global community.* Ensure there is local representation in the team you assemble who are given the jurisdiction to implement and revise the plan according to how it evolves in that location. Connecting back to the central hub can not only ensure there are common threads, but can also provide opportunities to share successes and try different approaches in other locations.
- *Use your plan as a guide, but revise, revise, revise!* I can't stress this enough. While there is some weight in the old adage 'fail to plan, plan to fail', there is also a lot of sense in the Burns' line 'the best laid plans of mice and men oft go awry'. I am constantly surprised by how many organisations cling hopelessly to plans that are failing. The plan is a foundation and a guide, but, when it comes to people, behaviour and culture, to reach your goals you must let it evolve organically. People, by their very nature, are unpredictable (just look at how often election polls are wrong) and understanding the beauty of this is how you will create within the community a sense of belonging. Unexpected outcomes of an action are often the thing that will help you to understand how the plan needs to evolve and, in doing so, lead you closer to where you want to be. Think like an entrepreneur, grasp the unexpected opportunities and don't be afraid to change direction (YouTube started out as a video-dating site). This approach also gives a sense of the community being developed for and by the employees, rather than a plan that is being imposed.

Assembling the team

Communities are led in very different ways from organisations. For example, in communities, there is shared accountability rather than hierarchy. In larger organisations, there is normally a head of D&I, with a team that sits beneath them, while, in smaller organisations, there may be just one person dedicated to D&I, relying on a steering committee to progress the agenda (which doesn't always happen as it very often slips off the radar outside of meetings once they are back doing their day jobs). How you assemble your team, which we can think of as the community 'hub', will be very much dependent on the size, maturity and culture within the business. Some points to consider:

- Is there a current D&I team in situ? How far does this team serve the purpose of a focus on belonging? How can it be evolved?
- If you are a global organisation, how will you ensure the plan is embedded in the regions? Do you have the resources to have a dedicated person in the location? If not, could the role be fulfilled by a team of senior leaders in each location to form a 'belonging' committee?
- Who else do you need to include to implement the plan? For example, how will you engage HR and communications?
- Finally . . . *make sure the team is diverse*! You need as many differing perspectives as you can, and employees in the wider organisation must feel that there is a voice in the team that understands their day-to-day experiences.

When considering those you want to involve or recruit to be part of the team, what are you looking for? I have personally found traits similar to those Kirsty Bashforth describes in her book *Culture Shift: A Practical Guide to Managing Organizational Culture* work best. Essentially, Kirsty describes disregarding skills or other criteria and focusing on those 'who have a passion for this sort of thing'. She describes six traits to look for:

- passion
- perception
- patience
- pedantry
- pragmatism
- pig-headedness.

Though seemingly disparate, to my mind, these combined traits are about energy. You want people who won't give up, who get things done, who aren't afraid to challenge the status quo, who will keep turning over stones until they find what they need and who keep going, even when there are setbacks or when progress is slow. They may be difficult to identify, but, when you find them, they are worth their weight in gold. And never stop looking for them. As you engage with the wider organisation, look out for these traits and bring those demonstrating passion into the team. Traits like these are not fixed – and, as your team grows, you will find they are infectious.

Signalling the plan to the wider organisation

Yet again, I am suggesting you buck the trend when it comes to communicating the change to the wider organisation. Communications and D&I teams spend countless days and weeks carefully crafting messages, briefing leaders, perfecting the communication from the CEO and signalling the incredible changes that they are about to deliver for the good of the organisation. (I am not criticising anyone for this, as I too have done the same . . .) Some employees ignore the communication altogether, others roll their eyes, while others, optimistic that something might finally change, are once again disappointed when the plan delivers lacklustre results. If you want to avoid the eye-rolling and 'here we go again' attitude, consider a different approach:

- If you have buy-in from the CEO, craft a communication that includes the headline results from the audit. The focus again should be on how the CEO feels about the data, what makes them proud, ashamed, angry or concerned, followed by their commitment to backing an approach that will ensure that everyone in the organisation feels that they belong.
- If there are structural changes to the organisation, for example if a central community function is being set up, explain in a communication what these will be to allay any concerns and ensure that you have briefed anyone who will be affected directly by the changes thoroughly before the wider communication is made.
- Keep it simple. Employees don't need bells and whistles, plans or detail. They need to feel the changes that happen. They need to feel that this time is different. So, ensure that the communication is given just before any activities or initiatives are launched, so it is clear early on that you mean business.

Assessing and implementing changes within the employee lifecycle

Doing a process review

Working with HR to review people processes within the employee lifecycle helps you to identify tweaks that will support belonging and the implementation of the plan. In addition, standards for future process development should ensure that they are sense-checked to ensure they support belonging and inclusion.

Recruiting a diverse workforce

If you Google 'Hiring diverse talent', you will find there are, at the time of this writing, 37,100,000 results. With this amount of information out there, there still seems to be slow progress in organisations bringing diversity into their talent pipeline through recruitment. Why is this? And what can practically be done to hire a more diverse talent pool?

There are some basic steps that can help you to get started, first in attracting diverse talent. But, before you jump in, ask yourself the question – what does diverse talent mean? As human beings, we like to be able to categorise and, until recently, the focus on hiring diverse talent has largely focused on gender, race and disability – simple categories that are easy to identify and measure. But diversity is so much more than this and, if organisations want to truly benefit from diversity, they must embrace the complexity and increasing intersectional nature of diverse identities. This means broadening the scope to:

- gender identity
- race/ethnicity
- religion
- level of education
- perceived social class
- disability
- neurodiversity
- work experience
- age.

And, in a rapidly evolving environment, where some people are experiencing significantly increased disadvantage, the conversation is turning to those with intersectional identities who tend to be absent from the diversity discussion. For example:

- BAME graduates are significantly less likely to be in full-time employment than white graduates.
- Graduates with a disability and those from more disadvantaged backgrounds are less likely to be in employment.
- Female graduates are paid 10 per cent less than male graduates.
- Young black men are more likely to have a criminal record than young white men, and black men with a record are less likely to be offered a job than white men with a record.
- 30 per cent of those who have served a prison sentence have ADHD and a criminal conviction is a major impediment to employment.

So, before you embark on changing the attraction and recruitment processes, you have to ask yourself:

- Are we willing to be transparent about recruitment data, processes and graduate salaries?
- Do we have commitment from the leadership team and legal team for 'fair-chance hiring' of those with a criminal record?
- Are we willing to do a deep-dive analysis into the recruitment processes, activities and data about how diversity-proof our current practices are?

Once you are ready to get started, here are some of the ways you can start to recruit a truly diverse talent pool:

- Inclusive language and accessibility:
  - Avoid 'gender-coding' – overly masculine or feminine language.
  - Consider literacy and dyslexia inclusion.
  - Avoid industry jargon to ensure you attract applicants with transferrable skills.
  - Consider how descriptions may inadvertently deter applicants from marginalised groups.
- Job descriptions:
  - Ensure job descriptions are specific to the requirements of the job.
  - Avoid using phrases such as 'and other ad-hoc activities'.
  - Be clear and concise.
- Person specifications:
  - Distinguish between skill and ability to attract those who don't have significant experience. Be clear on the level of experience required and how this might have been gained. Don't specify number of years' experience.

- Ensure requested qualifications and knowledge are genuinely required or whether the role could be met by specific skills and abilities without them.
- Be specific – for example, rather than 'strong communication skills', relate it to the actual requirements of the role, such as 'Ability to design materials for press briefings'.
- Never use personality traits, such as 'team player' or 'extrovert'.
- Broaden your network and recruit through diverse channels:
  - Find channels where you can target specific marginalised groups.
  - Broaden your network to those that include under-represented groups.
  - Partner with colleges, support groups or those that redeploy those with criminal convictions.
- Offer targeted internships and scholarships:
  - Work with the community to provide scholarship opportunities for those in disadvantaged or under-represented groups.
  - Offer paid internships to allow disadvantaged groups to gain experience and develop skills.
- Blind recruitment:
  - Remove all elements of applications that could identify identities that are most likely to be disadvantaged – for example gender, education, names, age, etc.
- Consider assessment activities:
  - Make sure reasonable adjustments are made for those who may need them – for example meeting the differing needs of neurodivergent candidates.
  - Consider why certain elements of the process are included. For example, including presentations can disadvantage differing personality types, levels of experience, those with some chronic illnesses/conditions and have been found to advantage male candidates.
  - Ensure you have a truly diverse recruitment and decision-making channel.
- Teach those involved in recruitment how to avoid bias:
  - Make sure all of those involved in recruitment see *all* recruitment as inclusive.
  - Provide training on the specific biases that can impair fair judgement in recruitment processes.
  - When it comes to decision making, have a checklist to ensure all biases have been checked and encourage the panel to challenge one another.

Onboarding

This is where the majority of organisations miss the opportunity to create a strong sense of belonging from day one. The majority of onboarding processes are 'done' to new starters. There is an attempt to indoctrinate the company purpose, culture and values, perhaps the opportunity to be presented to by some of the organisation's key players and, perhaps, some sheep-dip procedural or skills training. It is impersonal, creates little value and is company- rather than employee-centric.

A case study featured in the *Harvard Business Review*[1] describes research undertaken in a call centre in Wipro BPO, a business outsourcing centre in India. This industry has annual turnover rates of about 50–70 per cent and employees burn out quickly, mainly because they are encouraged to adopt Western accents and attitudes – in other words, to deny their own identity. In the study, the organisation split a new intake of employees into two. One group had the traditional company-centric onboarding experience, while the other went through an employee-focused programme. This experience included sessions on problem solving, helping individuals to understand their strengths and consider how these could be applied in their roles. Having the chance to share these with others in the group and to be able to be their authentic selves led to enduring collaboration between the employees and a 33 per cent reduction in staff turnover at six months into the role.

The onboarding process should be designed to demonstrate the sense of community and encourage the characteristics of 'My castle' – agency, curiosity and open-mindedness. It should be owned by the community team, with input, where required, from HR. When building your onboarding programme, consider things such as the following:

- As with Wipro, make your onboarding programme employee-centric, giving new starters the opportunity to explore their strengths, values and purpose in the context of and aligned to the organisation, as well as their individual roles.
- Share stories from existing employees about the organisation and their experiences within it – this will probably prove more motivating than hearing from leaders whose own experiences may not resonate with more junior employees.
- Spark curiosity and agency by getting the group to shape elements of the onboarding programme. Who would they like to hear from or meet? What would they like to find out more about and how? If they were to reshape the organisational values, what would they do? Collaboration from new starters who are looking at the organisation with a fresh pair of eyes could provide useful insights and ideas for the wider organisation.

- In the first few days, leaders should give each team the opportunity to get to know one another independently by giving them something to create or a problem to solve together. This will give the team a quick start in understanding how the team will evolve organically with the addition of the new employee.
- Give all new starters the opportunity to discuss ways of working that enable them to perform at their best. This may include where and when they work, reasonable adjustments for those with disabilities or neurodivergent conditions or something more specific to an individual.

Career progression and development

Learning and development

So, I am going to get this out of the way and I cannot stress it enough.

Do not do unconscious bias and diversity training.

Don't do it. And, if you are doing it, stop it. It isn't just that it doesn't work (which has been demonstrated over and over again), but it can, in fact, be divisive. It brings in the fierce rhetoric from both sides regarding systemic discrimination, which is being seen in the culture wars playing out in wider society today. If this happens, the belonging culture fails. Organisations have been using this as a compliance tool to mitigate risk should there be discrimination allegations. It is lazy, disingenuous and smacks of the lip service many organisations pay to D&I. Simply raising awareness of something does not impact intent-action, so it serves little purpose other than to protect the organisation. So, I am going to say it again.

Do not do unconscious bias and diversity training.

So, what *should* you do? Belonging and inclusion messages need to be weaved into all learning initiatives. Behaviour change is driven by context and repetition. Unconscious bias impacts our judgement in all areas – setting apart as a trait that primarily impacts discrimination sends the wrong message. I use judgement bias when talking about feedback, encouraging people to sense check their opinions against a range of potential biases before sharing. The process of doing this increases understanding of all biases and creates a habit of sense checking our judgements – *this* is what bridges intent-action.

I worked with The London Stock Exchange Group to develop a set of key belonging and inclusion messages that could be weaved into all learning and development initiatives. These messages were posed as questions designed to encourage employees to regularly pause, consider inclusive practice and test their judgement. These questions were:

- What don't I know and what assumptions am I making?
- Am I disempowering anyone with my actions?
- How might my actions impact the lived experience and happiness of all colleagues?

So, for example, within the context of recruitment training:
Question 1: What don't I know and what assumptions am I making?

- Challenge your assumptions when considering candidates for interview.
- If a candidate has disclosed a condition that is classed as a disability, do I know what adjustments should be made for the interview process?
- During the interview or afterwards, what biases might be affecting your judgements? What assumptions or suppositions are you making?

Question 2: Am I disempowering anyone with my actions?

- Inclusion means everyone. What aspects of the process might disempower certain people? Think about cultural differences and personality types, for example. How diverse are the group involved in the decision making and what impact might that have?
- Have you used inclusive language throughout the process? Have you used a variety of different channels to attract diverse talent?
- Ensure that evaluation is according only to the role you are recruiting for. Considering who has 'cultural fit', might 'fit in the team', or people you personally connect to, are the reasons why there is lack of diversity in many organisations.

Question 3: How might my actions impact the lived experience and happiness of all colleagues?

- If you make an offer to a candidate from a marginalised or under-represented group, are you confident that they would describe the recruitment process as positive and inclusive?
- How can you increase your awareness of inclusive practice and how processes impact those from marginalised groups?

Notice how the language in the questions is not restricted to marginalised or minority groups, including things such as, for example, personality differences. This shifts the focus to belonging for everyone as best practice, rather than something that should be considered only in specific groups of employees.

Leadership development

Stop talking about inclusive leadership. If your organisation has promoted somebody to a leadership position and they are not inclusive, then it is promotion criteria you should look at rather than leadership. These programmes actually stop the conversation around belonging and inclusion. They create a complexity that means leaders fear repercussions of getting it wrong, rather than the motivation to make everyone feel included, so they choose inaction as the safest option. Within the context of a belonging culture, as outlined previously in the framework, the focus of leadership development should be on facilitating the talent and well-being of everyone. So, rather than inclusive leadership as a sheep-dip approach for development, think of creating modular programmes that look at the behaviours that underpin this facilitative leadership. For example:

- leading with curiosity
- courageous conversations
- mental health first aid
- team well-being
- empowering others
- storytelling.

With this modular approach, you can create open-access resources, and activities open to the whole organisation, for very little cost, in addition to standard things, such as online learning, open-access panel discussions with an opportunity to pose questions on these subjects, increase awareness, stimulate discussion and spark curiosity. With many of my clients, I use something called 'nudge emails', which are sent out on a regular basis. These emails have a title posed as a question, designed to spark thinking. For example:

'Are you maximising your curiosity?'

Even if this is the only engagement an employee has with the communication, simply reading the title would have instigated some thinking. However, in every programme where these emails have been used, the email open rate has been extremely high. The email body then uses a magazine-style template to present things, such as links to videos, podcasts or articles, recommendations for books or apps, short bite-size 'explainers' and ideas for activities to try out. As well as embedding behaviours and creating habits based on programmes delivered, this low-cost scalable activity means they can be sent to anyone.

These widescale activities are not only great for development of a belonging culture, but also start to develop belonging leadership behaviours long before an employee is actually in a leadership role.

Education for understanding

There are some areas where it is necessary to provide education specific to diversity or certain minority groups, but these areas pertain mainly to specific roles or groups. For example:

- Diversity training for HR that allows for development of the policies that comply with legal obligations. It is also necessary for leaders to understand these policies.
- Cultural awareness training for those whose roles cross geographical boundaries where understanding of differences is critical to their success, for example sales people who work across global territories and must respect the customs and cultures to ensure they engage with clients successfully.
- Neurodiversity training or information available to all, and compulsory for managers and leaders. Neurodiversity is a complex area and one that tends to be poorly understood by those who have no experience within it (I have ADHD and, when I share this with people, many look perplexed. I can almost hear their brains trying to compute why there is a 9-year-old boy in front of them dressed as a 40-something woman . . .). As well as being a characteristic protected by the Equality Act, understanding from team mates and line managers can help ensure the employee is enabled to be the best they possibly can be.

Allyship

Many organisations now are focusing on developing allyship across the workforce and providing guidance or training for employees who self-select to become an ally. Allyship means creating an inclusive environment where different intersectional identities can advocate, sponsor, support and seek to understand the experiences of those in marginalised groups who may be disadvantaged. Organisations foster allyship through things such as:

- Continuous education on implicit bias, micro-aggressions and inclusive language – this is not 'one hit will do' training. This is a journey to re-wire connections in the brain, so it takes time, repetition and effort. As described earlier, key messages around these issues should be weaved into all development programmes rather than rolling out standalone programmes.

- Sponsorship programmes where employees can champion the career of a potentially disadvantaged colleague.
- Setting up reverse mentoring for leaders, pairings based on difference on a rolling basis to help leaders understand the lived experiences of a range of under-represented employees.

How can you become an ally?

As an individual, you have to commit yourself to being an ally. Genuinely commit. Walk the walk. Get out of your comfort zone. Be prepared to admit both ignorance and privilege. It takes hard work and perseverance. It is not a destination – it is a lifelong commitment to making sure you do all that you can to ensure the inclusion of those who may be marginalised in the workplace.

Do your homework

I don't mean Google ally and follow the instructions. You need to become a scholar, on a quest for understanding the lived experience of discrimination and exclusion. You need to roll up your sleeves and dig deep. Go back in history to understand the origins of discrimination that continue to underpin systemic disadvantage in many societal institutions today. You need to see the things that others don't (or won't). You need to feel uncomfortable and ashamed. You must ask difficult questions and continue to ask them over and over again, throughout your life. You need to immerse yourself so deep that you feel compelled to act and shout out, 'Not on my watch.'

Amplify the voices of those who are marginalised

Those who don't have a voice need others to give it to them and open up the floor for their opinions. Look out for those who are not being heard in any given situation and call it out. Bring those who are marginalised into the conversation and call out those who are leaving them out of it. Where you can, provide as many platforms as possible to allow under-represented opinions to be heard or expressed in a way that is comfortable for a broad range of personalities. Most importantly, when you agree with the expressed opinions, say it. Shout it and encourage others to do so.

Use your power to advocate for under-represented colleagues

Look around your networks, groups, regular events and prestigious or exclusive 'circles'. Who is under-represented? Who misses out on the opportunities these interactions create? Invite them in, take them along, bring them into the fold and encourage others to do the same. In conversations with those from marginalised groups, ask what opportunities they think they miss out on and where they would like to be included – after all, they are better positioned to recognise where the disadvantages lie. Then do whatever you can to create opportunity for them – and, if you can't, then introduce them to someone who can.

Be an upstander

This is the bit that takes courage – but, once one person starts, the commitment spreads. An upstander is the opposite of a bystander. Bystanders are those who may say they believe in inclusion for all but fail to intervene when they see contrary behaviours in action. Prejudice, discrimination, exclusion, oppression, persecution and bullying will continue to manifest where everyone chooses to be a bystander. Make your space one in the world within which you call out even the most minor of aggressions – you will be amazed how others follow suit and the difference you can make to the lived experience of the disadvantaged.

Earn the privilege of being a trusted confidante

Being an ally doesn't mean you are suddenly the new best friend of all those around you who may be disadvantaged. Even committing yourself to all of the above actions is not enough. Trust is about the predictability of behaviour over time and how others perceive their interactions with you. Being a confidante means allowing people the safety and space to tell you about their experiences of exclusion without being judged. The trust builds where you question, listen, seek to understand thoughts, feelings and, if a negative experience is based on their interaction with you, by not being defensive. Being a trusted confidante means acting with integrity always, admitting mistakes and caring personally about the lived experiences of those who are disadvantaged.

Sponsorship

Diversity and inclusion discussions have started to feature the idea of sponsorship as an activity within organisations to support the progress of minority or marginalised employees. However, there still seems to be confusion about the nature of sponsorship and how to go about it. In particular, many programmes reflect the nature of a mentoring relationship, rather than sponsorship. So, what's the difference and why should you focus on sponsorship?

In a mentoring relationship, the mentor helps the mentee to develop by providing advice and giving them insights from their own career and experiences. Mentoring relationships are sometimes within, or external to, organisations, may last for a fixed period of time or endure for many years. Sponsorship, on the other hand, is professionally driven. The benefits to individuals and cultures within organisations can be huge – but it is not an easy thing to do.

With sponsorship, a lot more is at stake – becoming a sponsor literally means that you are willing to put your professional reputation on the line for someone else. As a sponsor, you are professionally and emotionally invested in giving the employee their 'big break'. This means using your power, network and influence to drive career progress through things such as involvements in projects outside of the individual's roles, backing them for promotion or helping to build their profile at senior levels within the organisation. While these relationships are created within the organisation, it may also involve introductions to external networks to build a thought leader profile.

With this considered, it is critical that the selection and matching process is watertight. Get it wrong and two reputations could be on the line – and it isn't going to do the culture and brand much good either. This is the risky bit – and probably why most organisations opt for mentoring programmes instead. But, if you get it right, the impact on diversity is unprecedented – a future-proof way to start building more diverse senior leadership teams.

So, what do you need to consider?

First, you need to make sure there is no bias in selecting the junior talent pool. This means doing a deep dive into all aspects of the process and considering how the assessment process may disadvantage different under-represented groups.

Second, the process of talent selection and sponsorship has to be in line with what the employee wants. In an attempt to demonstrate progress by numbers, there has been a recent increase in what I describe as 'fast-dragging' – selecting talent based on the PR 'value' of their profile, for example Asian women in tech, then opening opportunities for advancement, which they may not necessarily want. Anyone entering into a sponsorship relationship has to be 100 per cent committed to advancing their career.

In terms of matching, consideration should be given first to where people are in the organisation. It is important that the sponsor is really familiar with the employee's work and believes in their potential. It may, therefore, be tempting to match within functions or business units, but this may limit the exposure to, and opportunities within, the wider organisation. Each individual case will be different but it is important to consider both of these things.

In terms of profiles of talent and sponsor (race, gender, LGBTQIA, etc.), some organisations try to match the two. The benefit of this is shared lived experiences, which the sponsor can help the employee to navigate. However, this may limit the supply of the number of sponsors, given the very nature of under-representation! There is also some benefit to matching diverse profiles to increase understanding, but, if this is the case, there has to be a good understanding by both within the relationship of the impact of 'similarity bias'. The relationship should allow both to be comfortable with being different – and the sponsor should recognise that the employee may have a very different leadership style and is not obliged to mirror that of the sponsor.

To realise the benefits of sponsorship programmes, start small, learn from the success of each relationship and make changes iteratively. Once you start seeing the benefits, the risks of this particular minefield will have been worth it.

Reverse mentoring

Reverse mentoring is the opposite of mentoring. It is not about the experienced imparting wisdom to the inexperienced, but where mentor and mentee are matched to increase understanding of differences – essentially, those who would normally be the mentor become the mentee. Senior leaders can be matched with junior employees, with those from marginalised groups or with those who have come from other industries, for example. The benefits of reverse mentoring schemes include:

- greater connectivity between different groups, which may not occur organically, leading to greater innovation
- understanding of differences, which promotes diversity and increases a sense of belonging
- allowing the sharing of skills across generations and insights between industries
- helping leadership decision making regarding product/service by creating understanding of more diverse customer segments
- supporting the organic development of shared purpose and values.

As with all mentoring programmes, there should be training provided for mentor and mentee prior to engagement to understand their role in the relationship, but, with reverse mentoring, greater consideration should be given to the following:

- Developing trust for both mentor and mentee, as they may both fear they will be exposed in the process. This means there should be clear objectives for the process, as well as clarification regarding the confidential nature of the relationship.

- Ensuring the mentee understands and is fully committed to their role in the process. Meetings should be prioritised and not regularly be cancelled or rescheduled – this will have a negative impact on the mentee as it signals that they are not valued. The mentee also has to be emotionally committed to learning from the process or they may be tempted to take control (as senior leaders are apt to do!) and flip the mentor–mentee relationship.
- Matching should be based on difference, based on where the mentee has specified a desire for greater understanding.

Performance management

As I am sure you have come to accept, my views on performance management are somewhat contrary to tradition. While many are looking for new approaches because we all know that it is a broken system, my view is that we scrap it altogether.

Could there ever be a less human term than 'performance management'? It has something of a machine feel to it and totally ignores the individuality of every employee. The machine feel has given way to processes riddled with bias and frameworks that require unfaltering conformity, as well as unrealistic expectations. For growth, innovation, equity and well-being to thrive in a belonging culture, I would recommend considering the following:

- Competency frameworks are the enemy of innovation and agility.
- Behaviour frameworks are the enemy of individuality and talent.
- If you want a belonging culture, scrap individual bonuses.
- Feedback is very rarely a gift.
- Performance reviews create complexity and bias – and they don't even work.
- Redefine and develop the role of the leader.
- Create a community charter.

Competency frameworks are the enemy of innovation and agility

Obviously, there are some skills and qualifications that are a pre-requisite to a given role and I am not suggesting we stop communicating those. What I am talking about are skills and, particularly, attributes that are fixed because, from experience, they are what has worked in the role. So, my point is this: how can we innovate if we only look back to what has worked in the past? Innovation, by its very nature, is unfixed, bringing together differing skills, ideas and capabilities that haven't been brought together before to create something that solves a problem for now and the future. Competency frameworks demand compliance to and measurement against a fixed set of skills, which is utterly illogical in an economy where innovation is king.

Behaviour frameworks are the enemy of individuality and talent

Behaviour frameworks fly in the face of the nature of talent and diversity. Take, for example, leadership frameworks (by the way, all of which are exactly the same wherever you go but are just word-smithed to sound different). For an organisation to be both inclusive and innovative, there must be diverse thinking in leadership teams. This diverse thinking should be made up of leaders who have strengths and talents in different areas. Using a behaviour framework as a measure of performance implies that great leaders are generalists who are skilled within a whole range of talents. Not only is this unrealistic, but it also has the potential to develop leadership generalists and mediocre, homogenous leadership teams who lack the ability to innovate. Measure and reward people on the development and application of their strengths, as well as awareness of and strategies to mitigate the risks of their weaknesses. After all, mavericks tend to be the greatest innovators and good all-rounders rarely go down in history.

If you want a belonging culture, scrap individual bonuses

Organisations, obsessed with the need for collaboration, literally put up a wall to prevent it from happening by continuing to focus on individual bonuses. This does two things, which contradict the values of a belonging culture. First, it allows employees to relentlessly pursue their own interests rather than collaborate with others to achieve common goals. Second, it creates a competition culture, which is the antithesis of collaboration. The achievement of the goal trumps the values of the organisation, which individuals may gladly flout, if contradictory behaviours can help them to achieve their goal. If you are going to keep an element of individual performance-related pay, then make sure it is less than 50 per cent of the overall sum – then the energy to achieve goals is focused in a way that supports a culture of belonging.

Feedback is very rarely a gift

Another of my much-hated phrases. In fact, I have a problem with the word feedback altogether, as, once again, it seems more appropriate when referring to machines. When someone utters the words, 'Can I give you some feedback?' (because the pithy acronyms often mention that you should always ask permission), it always reminds me of when somebody uses the passive-aggressive, 'With all due respect . . . ' (flagging that they are just about to disrespect you). Neuroscience research has shown that even mention of the word feedback elicits a stress response, which can increase the heart rate by 50 per cent. This is because our limbic system, which is responsible for the threat-reward system, prepares to respond to a threat. This is called amygdala hijack and it temporarily blocks the brain's control system. In Figure 6.1, you can see the social elements, described by David Rock (2008) in the SCARF model,[2] which we may perceive to be threatened – essentially, it is a threat towards our psychological safety. If this is sustained over a period of time it can impact mental health and well-being.

Yet, despite the evidence against it for years and years (and still today), managers have been sent on course after course, equipping them with a whole package of tools, models and acronyms that are rarely implemented well in the real world and, if they are, most of the time, pretty badly. This is, in the main part, because of what I like to call 'dot-to-dot management', the dilution of complex social interactions to pithy acronyms that are supposed to magically lead to enlightenment and heightened performance.

Apart from the psychological perspective described above, there is a complexity to the dynamics between a manager and employee that means it is very difficult for either party to be entirely objective, unless there is a deep understanding and trust between the two. This may sound counter-intuitive, but if, as a manager, you give feedback to somebody without truly understanding that person or the situation, then your feedback is based entirely on your own judgement. Therefore, it is subjective. Objective means that you have no feelings about the feedback you are giving, that you are merely stating a fact. How can that be when there is an existing relationship between the two parties? How can

Figure 6.1 The SCARF model

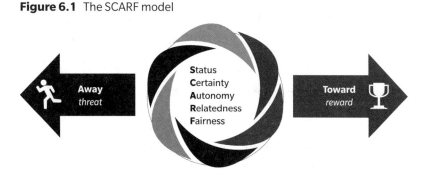

we possibly shut off the whole essence of being human simply because we are in an organisational setting?

Feedback should be left to computers, data and technology. People should have conversations. They should be kind, have integrity and seek to understand first. The same neuroscience research says that so-called 'feedback cultures' can develop only if control remains with the individual. This means that the individual should ask when they want feedback and it should always be solicited. The role of the leader is to create the psychological safety that will allow this to become the norm. It has to start at the very top with senior leaders requesting feedback regularly from employees at all levels. This role-modelling should trickle down through the organisation with management programmes leading on how to ask for, rather than how to give, feedback. In time, this behaviour among leaders will come to be seen as a norm and provide the psychological safety for the wider organisation to start doing the same. Once employees start to feel the reward for this behaviour in terms of their growth, it will become embedded into how they work and into the organisational culture.

That is how people develop and grow in a belonging culture.

Performance reviews create complexity and bias – and they don't even work

Performance reviews are the part of the system many leaders hide behind so that they don't have to have difficult conversations or think about the 'people stuff' throughout the year. It has become so embedded as a difficult, but necessary, procedure that the human element seems to have been stripped out of it completely. It is something that employees feel is 'done' to them, a process over which they have no control, yet are required to spend time preparing for anyway.

A 2019 Gallup survey of over 60 million employees found that, despite 91 per cent of organisations surveyed saying that they conducted annual performance reviews, only 14 per cent of employees said that they were inspired to improve as a result of them.[3]

In fact, a study published by the American Psychological Association[4] found that one third of the time it actually makes performance worse. In the words of Gallup, when they presented their research:

> '. . . if performance reviews were a drug, they would not meet FDA approval for efficacy.'

So, what can be done instead? How can we create belonging and still ensure performance is monitored and improved?

Redefine and develop the role of the leader

The role of the facilitative leader, as previously discussed, is to leverage the talent of all employees. This means that focus on performance and well-being is the priority with the role, therefore negating the need for protected times or processes to ensure it is managed. This means supporting, not judging.

The key is the leader's concern with developing deep understanding of each individual team member. This means the leader is more accurately able to understand what lies behind their performance and find opportunities to leverage their talent.

With this refocus of the leadership role, leaders are in a better position to identify appropriate performance goals and support any underlying challenges that may be impacting the behaviour of team members

Create a community charter

As discussed previously, communities don't prescribe behaviours to their members. They develop a set of values to which all members are committed and which means that the values become embedded in the way they behave. The way each person behaves might be very different, but, regardless, the ultimate goals and values are the same. Those who consistently don't uphold the values pretty quickly self-select out if they are in a significant minority or else the community asks them to leave.

This is no different from what organisations have been trying to achieve through frameworks, models, systems, projects, policies, platforms and consultants for years and years when the answer is simple. Being part of a community means the community promises you this and, reciprocatively, to be a part of it, the members promise this.

Focusing on a community charter, rather than a frameworks approach, retains the unique identity of the individuals within the organisation and beholds them to the promises they have made to uphold the values. It is simply the psychological contract that is often talked about as something allusive or intangible. For example:

- The organisation is committed to ensuring that we protect the well-being of all our employees.
- Our employees commit to ensuring they fully protect the well-being of their colleagues.
- If an employee behaves in a way that they have been told is having a negative impact on a colleague (which is a fact that cannot be disputed), as well as having been given guidance on how they can rectify it, but continues to behave in the same way, then they are not upholding the values of the organisation and, therefore, have broken the contract.

So, performance management or assessment in the context of a belonging culture asks two simple questions:

- Are you striving towards, and meeting, the goals that we have agreed together?
- Are you being an upstanding member of our community by upholding our values?

Exiting

People leaving the organisation is a fantastic opportunity for them to be frank about the experience of being employed there and for you to collect invaluable stories and data. People leaving is inevitable, but, as part of the organisational responsibility for employee well-being, leaving with a sense of belonging can be critical to both long-term well-being and a positive external employee brand. Evidence has shown that harassment and bullying in the workplace have a significant impact on well-being way beyond the experience itself. It can lead to prolonged physical health issues related to stress, mental health problems like anxiety, depression or even PTSD. Organisations must recognise this and understand that, in addition, a positive experience of belonging within the organisation can add value to employees' lives beyond their employment.

Global Community & Belonging at Brandwatch

The role of the community manager as one that manages communications into and out of the organisation via social media is a role that has started to become more prevalent over the past few years. Normally, sitting within the marketing function, community managers are the face of the company, pushing out content, creating dialogue and gaining insights through social media. More recently, some organisations have recognised there is an opportunity for a similar role to be implemented to build an internal community. As already discussed, community is a powerful mechanism for increasing diversity, by connecting to different external communities and belonging, by creating a strong internal community feel.

One such company is Brandwatch, a global digital consumer intelligence company, who have over 500 employees worldwide. Abadesi Osunsade is the first in the newly appointed role of VP of Global Community &

Belonging and, when I spoke with her, she had only been in the role for a few months, but was already having an impact and making impressive progress. One of the first things she did was to reach out globally to as many employees as she could to understand their values and concerns, to look for opportunities where the organisation could align. One such area she found was the concern about the advancement of technology and the need for the company to remain committed to ethical (artificial intelligence) AI in the future. Understanding this concern also provides insight as to how the brand may be perceived and the organisation can prioritise communicating its continuing commitment to ethical AI internally and externally, aligning organisational, customer and employee values.

In addition, in looking for ways to attract more diverse talent in a sector renowned for its homogeneity, Abadesi is connecting to external communities, such as People of Color in Tech, an approach that extends the idea of community beyond the organisation itself, and is also looking for how they can remove bias from all attraction and recruitment processes.

She says there are three key things that have allowed her to make such progress in such a short time:

- Being able to be her authentic self.
- Being trusted and empowered to set her own agenda.
- Absolute commitment from the Brandwatch CEO and his leadership team.

As a pioneer in this area, Abadesi's experience and insights show clearly how other organisations can be successful in implementing similar roles.

Changing hearts and minds

The so-called 'culture wars' in wider society are fostering increasing polarisation when it comes to views on discrimination, and some of these attitudes are being reflected within organisations. In driving the plan forward, you may have to counter some of these attitudes along the way:

- 'White men are blamed for everything.'
- 'Why should some people be given advantage over others?'
- 'Quotas are unfair. Recruitment and promotion should be based on competence and merit.'
- 'Why are we spending money on this? There is no racism or other discrimination in the organisation.'
- 'Here we go again . . . ' [eye roll].

Keeping the communication change simple and focusing on the need to make everyone feel that they belong will help allay some of the usual objections, but these are some of the attitudes you will encounter along the way when you start implementing the plan. Deal with these as follows:

- Engage in the conversation by genuinely asking questions about the concerns to try to understand them. One of the biggest mistakes where there is polarity is that conversations are shut down, which serves only to increase the differences. The people who have the concerns are part of the community and, to feel that they belong, they must also be heard.
- As far as you can, respond to the concerns directly, for example recruitment processes are focused on attracting diverse applicants and enabling everyone to showcase their talents as best as they possibly can, but the decision regarding selection will always be made on who is best for the job.
- Bring the attention back to the concept of community, that the approach is designed to leverage the talents and protect the well-being of all employees so that everyone can be the best they can be.
- Anywhere extreme views or values contrary to a sense of community are expressed, which they may well be, given the rhetoric around freedom of speech in wider society, make it clear that they are entitled to their personal opinions but that these do not have a place within the organisation. Reiterate the concept of belonging, community and well-being, making it clear, in no uncertain terms, that any expressed views (directly or indirectly) that make any other employee uncomfortable about who they are have no place within the organisation.

Notes

- -

1 Cable, D., Gino, F. and Staats, B. (2015) 'The Powerful Way Onboarding Can Encourage Authenticity', 26 November.

2 Rock, D. (2008) 'SCARF: A brain-based model for collaborating with and influencing others.' *NeuroLeadership Journal*, Issue One.

3 Wigert, B. and Harter, J. 'Re-Engineering Performance Management' available at: https://www.gallup.com/workplace/238064/re-engineering-performance-management.aspx?thank-you-report-form=1

4 Kluger, A.N. and DeNisi, A. (1996) 'The effects of feedback interventions on performance: A historical review, a meta-analysis, and a preliminary feedback intervention theory', *Psychological Bulletin*, 119(2), 254–84. Available at: https://doi.org/10.1037/0033-2909.119.2.254

chapter 7

Help your employees to thrive at work

Wellness and well-being initiatives have been gathering pace in many organisations, though, for many, it is still very much in its infancy. Within a community context, there is collective responsibility for the welfare and, in this chapter, I will explore ways in which this can be supported:

- how the organisation-community can support the well-being of all employees
- additional considerations for leaders regarding team well-being in a virtual world
- the responsibility of leaders and employees to speak up on behalf of their colleagues
- how organisations can help employees to thrive by creating connections

Well-being – one size does not fit all

The outdated, corporate blanket approach to so many initiatives does not work – it wastes money, benefits no one and wastes time, as functions use tangential data to demonstrate their success to leadership teams. As well-being and wellness programmes become more popular, organisations are falling into this same trap again.

To take a belonging approach to this subject, organisations have to admit that the experience, circumstances and attributes of each employee are entirely unique. The blanket approach is unlikely to provide any real benefit for the majority of the organisation. Leaving aside all the corporate well-being/wellness speak, this subject needs to come down to a human level. Research has shown that the strong sense of belonging fostered in communities contributes to, and is considered the collective responsibility of, the well-being of all. In turn, this creates community 'vitality' – greater engagement and a willingness to act for the good of the community. The organisation-community can benefit from this by applying the principles of the Belonging Framework and by providing holistic support to ensure that everyone, without exception, can thrive.

An organisation's approach to thriving should extend way beyond the context of the formal structure and should support thriving in all areas of an employee's life. Thriving must be considered holistically and, if the employee isn't thriving in their personal life, they will struggle to thrive at work. When they are not thriving at work and are having to keep personal problems entirely separate, they will not feel a sense of belonging. Essentially, the organisation-community should *encourage* employees to bring their problems to work! As we have seen, this is particularly pertinent as virtual working is increasing exponentially and the boundaries between home and work are becoming less discernible. Any personal problems or mental health issues that go unresolved, regardless of the cause, are likely to result in lost productivity. The organisation-community should provide a range of resources that employees can utilise confidentially, when it is required. This might include, among other things:

- financial management advice and education
- fitness and diet
- stress management
- relationships and family support
- support for carers
- bereavement and loss
- chronic illness support
- access to medical services.

This need not be costly if you are a small business, as it can be as simple as a library of resources providing guidance on who can give advice or help outside of the organisation. There should be somebody in the organisation with whom employees can request to speak confidentially – this role should be independent, with their stated objective being solely to support employees and should, therefore, not be somebody in an HR role.

Larger organisations can choose to develop these resources internally within the organisation-community function or choose an external provider. Some employee benefit providers provide a suite of services to support the well-being and wellness of employees, their partners and children. For example, one provider has developed an app where employees can remotely access:

- remote clinician appointments
- mental health support via trained therapists or computer-based therapies
- a physiotherapy assessment and treatment plan
- a second opinion following final consultant diagnoses
- an employee assistance programme that provides life, financial and well-being support for employees and their families as well as access to a 24/7 help hotline.

However you provide support, the services will be effective only if employees believe it is entirely employee-focused and that there is complete confidentiality. A report entitled 'Mental health and employers: Refreshing the case for investment', published in January 2020 by Deloitte, suggested the reasons people don't seek help from organisations are largely because they are worried about confidentiality or because they want to keep the problem away from others in the organisation or formal processes (Figure 7.1).

Figure 7.1 If you didn't approach HR or Occupational Health, why is that?

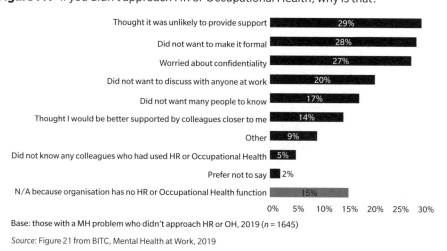

Base: those with a MH problem who didn't approach HR or OH, 2019 (*n* = 1645)

Source: Figure 21 from BITC, Mental Health at Work, 2019

To develop trust in the confidential nature of all interactions with these support services, organisations should:

- be clear in communicating why the organisation is doing this and why it is important
- mitigate cynicism by making it publicly known that the services operate without input from the wider organisation or executive team
- ensure the employees know that this is a confidential service and any data emerging from the activities, such as use of services, is always reported anonymously
- ensure that the approach of the team must not be sensitive to changes in business priority and the services must remain consistent. The only time there may be a change in tempo is in response to internal or external crises, which may mean the employees require enhanced support.

In addition, organisations should make a concerted effort to raise awareness and understanding of mental health issues in order to reduce the stigma that very often holds people back from reaching out for help, particularly in younger generations. Consider doing mental health awareness sessions as part of graduate or apprenticeship programmes so that younger employees are able to recognise signs of stress, depression and anxiety in both themselves and others.

Can well-being be measured?

CEO Edwyn van Rooyen is a firm believer in creating technology for the greater good – and it is thanks to entrepreneurs like him that we are seeing more technology-based solutions being developed to enhance well-being in an increasingly virtual world. Along with a diverse group of pioneers from a variety of fields, Edwyn developed an app, 'T-Cup', where individuals can track health, happiness and success through nine core areas of well-being. They can track progress, reach goals and more efficiently target areas that need improvement. In turn, the organisation has access to real-time, anonymous data, which allows them to provide the right support measures in response.

More and more technology like this is becoming available, providing a real-time wealth of understanding that, in turn, can support the strategic decisions that are put in place. This takes the guesswork out of targets, plans and activity, as it is the community itself, not the organisation, that defines how resources are assigned.

The beauty of this technology is that it provides real-time tailored, dynamic support for individuals in addition to benefitting the collective well-being of the wider organisation.

Thriving in a virtual world

The increase in virtual working, following the announcement of the COVID pandemic in 2020, whipped leaders and organisations into a frenzy as they wondered what on earth it meant for the leadership and people agendas. Cue a flurry of articles on how to lead in a virtual world, leading virtual programmes and surveys from management consultancies.

As belonging and well-being became critical priorities for ensuring business continuity, when real purpose had to provide connectivity rather than proximity in a physical office and where agility relied on the mental capacity of employees to be able to cope with speed and frequency of change, I was rather delighted as it signalled (seemingly, for the first time for some) that central to leadership is the individual employee – actual people with unique personalities and needs. To my mind, it sparked the opportunity for the most positive change in organisations' leadership approach since writing on the subject began in the 1960s.

The Belonging Framework, with a sense of community at the heart, is applicable to both the physical and virtual world and, moreover, is the change that will take organisations forward now and in the future. Placing identity firmly central means that the principles of the framework allow the organisation to adapt rapidly according to need while preserving the engagement, connectivity and well-being of all employees.

Creating shared purpose and connectivity in a virtual world

The Belonging Framework has purpose at the core of each of the principles and, while this, in essence, remains the same in the virtual world, communication channels to maintain a sense of purpose and create connectivity should be carefully thought through. The right technology platforms are critical for enabling communication, connectivity and seamless workflows, but technology does not in itself guarantee connectivity and shared purpose:

- Organisations and leaders should consider how they can create shared purpose and connectivity through ritual and routine. In times of fast-paced change, people look for aspects of the world with stability and certainty. For example, teams could start each week with a virtual breakfast then end it on Fridays with an online meeting. A quick 10-minute team meet every morning can help maintain the shared sense of purpose. This idea of ritual and routine can also apply to organisation-wide comms plans.

- Organisations should be creative about how they connect people to make up for the lack of 'water-cooler' moments. A client of mine hosts virtual coffee mornings where employees are randomly assigned to a short video conference where they get to know others from across the organisation and find out about projects that are going on in other areas.
- Emotional connectivity doesn't have to be all about technology. Knowing everyone is doing something at the same time creates a feeling of connectedness. Mid-afternoon is, apparently, when we are mostly likely to feel a sense of isolation, so encourage teams to collectively turn their attention to something different at this time.
- While the routine creates the certainty, ensure that team communication doesn't become monotonous by using different ways to communicate. While video conferencing (VC) is becoming the norm, leaders should be aware of VC fatigue . . . sometimes, a simple chat on the phone may be a welcome relief.

Protecting well-being in the virtual world

Connectivity and purpose can help well-being, but, in the virtual world, leaders should make a conscious effort to stay vigilant to changes. One of the problems arising from virtual working is something that has been dubbed 'leaveism' – burnout and stress related to a feeling of being consistently 'on'. When home and work are the in the same place, it is important for organisations and leaders to ensure that employees create boundaries between work and personal time.

- Leaders must be aware of individual circumstances and not make assumptions about changes in engagement, productivity or mood. People's attitudes towards virtual working vary and, indeed, for some, where perhaps home life has its own challenges, being there all the time can present specific difficulties. Leaders should start all one-to-one interactions by asking about the individual, not work, and end conversations with the question highlighted earlier: how can I make your life better?
- Have organisation or team rules based on rules of engagement and protecting personal time. Notice if somebody appears to be working or communicating significantly outside of work hours and ask why. Although this sort of flexibility works for some people, if it happens too much in a team or organisation, others can start to feel that they must conform to this 'norm'.
- Beware of tracking tools to monitor how efficiently people are using their time. Even Liam McIvor Martin, the CEO of work time tracking platform Time Doctor, has said, 'The biggest thing we need to track right now is mental health, not if people are getting a 5 per cent or 10 per cent productivity boost.'

Another issue regarding virtual working in the context of well-being is the feeling of isolation that some employees may experience. This is particularly true of employees who live alone, as the workplace often provides one of the most significant opportunities for social interactions they have – and, as we know, social interactions are a core part of our sense of belonging within a collective. Leaders should be aware of the ways in which interactions with team members may compound these feelings and ensure everyone in the team is aware too.

- Emotional sense-check all your communications (this is a good habit to get into anyway as a leader, but particularly where people are feeling isolated). So, let's say, for example, a team member sends you something they have been working on for a while. You take a look, it is good and now you have to plan how to move forward with it. You are busy, so send a quick email that says, 'Can you schedule some time with me over the next couple of days?' In the physical workplace setting, the team member may be having the conversation with you face to face, so you would (hopefully) have shared your opinion about the work before proceeding to talk about next steps. If not, the team member may turn to a colleague and share their concern about why you are requesting a meeting, the ensuing conversation perhaps helping them to think objectively about the response. Receiving such a message at home, when somebody is already feeling isolated, will almost certainly add to the burden of low mood or even impaired mental health. If you are unsure of how to construct a message or tone, pick up the phone. And *never* give negative feedback or bad news by email or any other written text.
- Support well-being and help to reduce feelings of isolation by encouraging team members to get out of the house for a walk each day. Getting outside when you have mental health issues is one of the most important things to do, but, unfortunately, one of the most difficult for those with a low mood. So, make it a team activity. I heard recently about a team who were telling employees to go for a walk every lunchtime – they launched this in winter, when it is dark at the end of the working day, knowing that the opportunity to get out into daylight must be during working hours. Each day, the team all shared a photo from their walk. A great initiative that both connects people, reducing feelings of isolation, and makes sure, for well-being's sake, that they get their all-important daily dose of UV rays.
- Facilitate employees checking in on one another. If you are a small team, it is simple enough to do this by all making a commitment to do so, but it is still possible if you are a much larger organisation. Social media platform management company Buffer does this by using a functionality within Slack, which pairs people automatically. They call it 'pair calls' – those who want to opt in are randomly paired with another employee once a week to chat about anything they want to.

A word on language

Whether you like it or not, what makes us human is the fact that we have and can express emotions. While we can all learn how to act with emotional intelligence, there is no one who is immune to low mood or mental health impairment. There are times when our mood or impairments make it difficult for us to control our responses, feelings or thoughts. I have both been subject to, and far too often witnessed, language that is so destructive in this context that it actually flies in the face of both emotional intelligence and supporting belonging. So, as a leader, commit to removing the following phrases, or any others like them, from your lexicon because they have never helped *anyone* and serve only to embed negative feelings:

- 'You are taking this too personally,' or its close relation, 'Why do you take everything to heart?'
- 'Stop being dramatic.'
- 'You can't take feedback.'
- 'Why are you being so emotional?'

These statements are wrong and destructive on so many levels that I barely know where to start.

- First, depression, by its very nature, causes sufferers to have alarmingly low self-esteem. While we all have an inner-critic, in depression it is persistent, loud and crippling. When we fear anything, we become hyper-vigilant to it. So, when somebody says something that could serve as external confirmation of these perceptions, the fight or flight response kicks in, causing a reaction. When you then criticise with this statement, you serve only to deepen the sense of self-loathing. It really is that serious. You never know how close to the edge someone with depression is and, likewise, those who suffer with depression are, more often than not, very good at keeping it hidden (consider the high incidence of depression in comedians and actors). You have no idea what consequences such words could have.
- You may not understand what is making somebody feel a certain way or causing them to react in a certain way. For example, I have ADHD, which frequently presents with depression and anxiety. Women or girls with ADHD are often described by others as 'drama queens' (these are the actual words used in medical texts). Why is this? Well, one potential reason is a challenge many people with ADHD have called Rejection Sensitive Dysphoria. Dysphoria means 'hard to bear' and, if a sufferer perceives a potential rejection cue, it triggers emotional responses that may seem disproportionate. Actually, they

are chemically experiencing the same heightened emotions others would feel in extreme distress. This is not within their control and, again, pointing out something that is, in fact, part of a disability is not only discriminatory but may also increase social anxiety and shame, while lowering self-esteem.

- Obviously, the condition described above is extreme compared to other people's reactions but you must remember that, when it comes to neurology, we are all different and, essentially, on a spectrum. Therefore, nobody can profess to understand the internal, emotional world of others and nobody has the right to declare a line in the sand that delineates between what is a normal and abnormal response.

- Accepting what you, and others, think and feel is OK is one of the fundamental cornerstones of emotionally intelligent leadership. Labelling a reaction with any of these phrases I have described is, potentially, destructive. A leader should seek to understand why somebody is reacting in a certain way and either clarify their intention or help the employee to consider the situation more objectively.

Collective responsibility for well-being – encouraging a speak-up culture

To be clear, before we start, when I talk about speaking up, I am not referring to whistleblowing, as this is an entirely different business ethics discussion, which I won't be dealing with in this context. I am talking about the moral proscriptions as given in the definition of the organisation as a community – speaking up, for oneself or on behalf of another person, if you see a behaviour in action that is contrary to creating a sense of belonging or the values of the organisation.

In their book *Speak Up*, Megan Reitz and John Higgins present research they conducted with around 1,000 managers. They asked the managers how good junior, mid-level and senior-level employees are at speaking up. Then they asked the managers how good they personally are at speaking up about misconduct. The results, as you can see below, are quite telling.

Junior employees	Mid-level employees	Senior-level employees	You (respondents)
50%	67%	73%	82%

Reitz and Higgins say that this data shows one of the reasons why people don't speak up – they are far too busy focusing on how bad others are at it, clinging to the belief that they are better than everyone else! Think about it. Have you ever been in a situation, a meeting, for example, where you have seen someone being aggressive towards someone else? Have you sat there thinking something along the lines of, 'Why isn't anybody saying anything? *What is wrong with these people?!*'? Or, after the meeting, said to the employee who was being targeted, something like, 'That was awful! They shouldn't be allowed to get away with that!' I think we are all guilty of this to a greater or lesser degree.

'Calling it out'

The key to encouraging a speak culture is in creating a psychological safety so that people feel that they can 'call it out' without fear of repercussions and this is a behaviour that must be role modelled by leaders. Leadership development should include programmes on leadership courage and courageous conversations so they develop the confidence to embed the behaviours in their ways of working. If a leader stands by when there is a demonstration of aggression contrary to the organisation's values, they essentially endorse the behaviour. 'Calling it out' may be appropriate in a variety of situations but need not be confrontational, which is why good role modelling is essential. It may be general, applying to situations where someone is aggressive or dismissive to another employee, or it may be more specific, relating to minority or marginalised groups.

Being an upstander

An upstander is, literally, the opposite of being a bystander. If you are passive in your role as a witness or bystander, then you are a part of the problem. One of the challenges is that those who are most likely to be the recipient of these behaviours are those most likely to have the least psychological safety, making it difficult for them to stand up for themselves. If this is a frequent occurrence, mental health and well-being can suffer. This really isn't acceptable and the only way to prevent anyone from feeling like this is for others to step in on their behalf. As I have said, leaders have the responsibility to role model this, as they have the advantage of being less likely to fear retaliation. In time, this gives others the psychological safety to step in, as their fear of retaliation is replaced by the knowledge that the behaviour is endorsed within the organisation.

Aggressions don't need to be overt to be harmful to a sense of belonging. Micro-aggressions, such as always asking the female in a meeting to take notes, or everyone picking up their phones as a colleague starts to present, must also be called out. Otherwise, the message is that some people have more value and worth than others.

IBM recently launched an online course and platform to help combat these aggressions and truly integrate the organisation's values. The course uses stories to help people to understand how a poor sense of belonging feels and provides guidance for how to be an upstander. In addition, they launched a platform called Talk It Over @IBM, which encourages anyone who witnesses, experiences or hears about behaviours contrary to the organisational values to speak up and say, 'This is not what IBMers stand for.' This is a simple, scalable and relatively low-cost solution that could make a big difference to the organisational culture.

Anti-racism

Despite the fact that the majority of people would say they are not racist, this has clearly not been enough to eliminate the systemic racism that is still deeply embedded in many of our society's institutions. The conversation has now turned to anti-racism. To be not racist is passive, whereas anti-racism is the active effort of opposing and working against the multi-dimensional mechanisms that serve to perpetuate racist ideas and actions in society. But, to do this, you must first commit yourself to understanding the origins of these mechanisms by looking back in history to see the origins of this oppression.

In many countries, the history books have been 'white-washed', excluding the presence of people of colour. A shared understanding of history is critical for us to start having conversations about race. For too long, we have casually and conveniently torn out these pages of the history books – both the stories that have caused pain and those that we should be celebrating. Understanding the origins of racial injustice will open our eyes to the elements that have travelled with us through history and, today, still feed both the privilege, experienced predominantly by white people, and the oppression, experienced by people of colour. Explicit and implicit racial injustice still exist and will continue to do so as long as we are not having conversations about race.

So, what can you do?

The issue of racial injustice requires understanding of not just an individual's perspective – to be 'anti-racist' you must commit fully to understanding the issue holistically and being part of the systemic change that is needed. Here is how you can get started:

- *Get comfortable with being uncomfortable*
  - Start with being uncomfortable with how little you actually understand.

- Acknowledge that it may be uncomfortable to hear about the pain of individuals related to the behaviours of others, as well as elements of the historical origins that endure today.
- Be prepared to deal with your own emotional responses as understanding increases and when challenging personal biases that you may find confusing.

- *Understand and acknowledge privilege*

  - Privilege can be defined as unmerited or unearned advantage.
  - Privilege comes from many sources – examining the history of racial injustice in your country helps to develop understanding of your own privileges.
  - To be part of the change, you must be willing to acknowledge and own the privilege, understanding how it manifests in racial injustice.

- *Commit to being part of the change*

  - Don't start the conversation until you have internalised what you have learned and reframed your perspective.
  - Don't have the conversation unless you are genuinely committed to taking action against racism.
  - Understanding the issue from an historical and human pain perspective will help you to approach the conversations with respect.
  - Explore the types of conversation you can have from water-cooler chats to opportunities for group learning.

You have probably heard of 'micro-aggressions' within the language of D&I, but let's flip the narrative and start using 'micro-moves'. This means being conscious of the fact that, while you can seek to understand and support marginalised colleagues, you can never truly understand their experiences. Conversations, therefore, require courage, humility and authenticity, as well as being contextual. So, for example, in an organisational setting, ask questions relating to something happening in the organisation, in wider society or something that the individual may have recently experienced. This may be:

- 'It is difficult for me to understand experiences you may have had so, I hope you don't mind me asking – what are your thoughts on unconscious bias training?'
- 'The Black Lives Matter campaigns are something most people feel they understand, but, unless it is a part of our identity or we have experienced any kind of oppression, I don't think we can profess to understand. I'd love to hear your views.'
- 'As a new starter, you have recently experienced our recruitment processes – do you feel the process was truly inclusive?'

But it also requires those asking the questions to be accepting of any response they get. Defensive, or seemingly aggressive reactions, should not illicit a defensive reaction. This is not personal and it is not about you. You have never lived their experiences and this is part of the journey to genuine inclusivity.

Thriving through purpose and meaning

'What man actually needs is not a tensionless state but rather the striving and struggling for some goal worthy of him. What he needs is not the discharge of tension at any cost, but the call of a potential meaning waiting to be fulfilled by him.'

Viktor Emil Frankl (1905–97)

We have looked at how purpose at an individual, team and organisational level is a fundamental element of the Belonging Framework, but, under difficult circumstances, it takes on even greater significance. Those who suffer with mental health problems often have a bleak sense of purpose and meaning. While, often, the world around them hasn't significantly changed, profound mental changes mean that their interpretation of it, and their existence within it, has. Sometimes, something in the world around them has changed, which then changes their interpretation of everything within it, despite the fact that most aspects have remained stable.

With this in mind, I believe that leaders and organisations have a huge societal responsibility to create as much stability and certainty for employees as they possibly can. Whether it be personal or environmental circumstances that are impacting the well-being of an employee, leaders can endeavour, at these times, to help employees to create meaning or refocus them on purpose in several ways:

- As described when I talked about language, don't judge perspective or emotion when an employee is sharing how they feel. Listen, acknowledge and thank them for sharing with you. Tell them that it must be very difficult for them at the moment but that they are supported. This often helps people to open up further about how they feel.
- Listening and paraphrasing to show that they are being heard is, in itself, supportive, but it also helps people to make sense of how they feel. You are not a therapist but every human being has the capacity to empathise (well, perhaps not all, but most).

- When someone is sharing how they feel with you, try to get them to link it to their values. So, for example, an employee says to you:

  'I am so exhausted right now; I can't think straight and I just feel like I am letting everyone else in the team down.'

  You can respond with:

  'I can understand why this is an added burden for you on top of everything else – you are somebody who always strives to help others so feeling that you aren't must be tough. We are here to support you because we all know that, if it is one of us, you would do the same.'

  This links the negative feeling to the fact that a core value and strength of the individual is being compromised. And that helps not just to create meaning of the situation, but also reminds them of a core part of their purpose within the team.

- You can also help by focusing the employee towards a task or action that highlights the purpose of the organisation and that gives meaning to the individual's role. This might be focusing on something to do with how customers benefit, or it might be connected to the way in which broader society benefits. If the employee is overwhelmed, keep it simple, reallocate complex or repetitive tasks and have them focus on applying their own strengths and values towards the purpose of their role. For example, as part of the senior leadership team at a vaccines company, I could create meaning and purpose for people by focusing on a task around trial outcomes and health improvements. Simply giving someone a task that focuses on purpose or allows them to see how their strengths create value can make a big difference. It goes a long way in supporting well-being, particularly when there is uncertainty in other areas of their life.

Thriving through connectivity

Increasing and strengthening the connections between employees can have a significant impact on well-being, belonging and engagement. This can be done in so many ways – as well as traditional activities, it is important to think beyond to other ways that can create a sense of connectedness in people.

Connecting through networks

Though often used interchangeably, there is a fundamental difference between networks and employee resource groups (ERGs) – networks are largely self-managing and serve the needs of their members, while ERGs usually have a formal structure prescribed by the organisation who benefits from the insights the group provides by applying them to external as well as internal decision making. I have a fundamental problem with the concept of an ERG as, to me, it flies in the face of empowerment, true diversity and community for the following reasons:

- In any community, everyone has to feel that they have a voice. While both networks and ERGs can provide this, ERGs can determine how, what and when this voice contributes. This somewhat dilutes empowerment.
- Everyone in a community is entitled to a safe space and this is what networks can provide – a place where employees can connect with others who have the same day-to-day experiences. While it is useful to have a sponsor for the purpose of connecting the network to the organisation and negotiating budgets for events, if too much control is exercised on behalf of the organisation, then it somewhat dilutes this safe space. Organisations often do this as they fear employee activism. Amazon, for example, has dismissed employee activists protesting against working conditions because they fear activism is a precursor to unionising, which would only happen in an organisation where employees are *not* given a voice. LGBTQ+ networks had enormous success in terms of corporate activism through networks by, for example, pushing for equal partner benefits.
- Unnecessary bureaucracy imposed from the top should be minimised in a community as it regulates the potential for innovation that self-organising presents.
- The organisation using insights from an ERG may be useful for the present but does not address the fact that these voices are not represented where decisions are being made. This should be the priority to which networks can contribute ideas.

Connecting through conversation and stories

One of the reasons loneliness exists today is because of the way in which people connect with one another. We might connect with people in teams around the work we do together or in networks because we share an aspect of identity.

Socialising tends to be online or in crowded noisy places. Jillian Richardson found this after she graduated and moved to New York:

> 'We used to have to rely on each other more. We had to be a part of a community to survive. It's so easy to lead individualistic lives now. We go to work, we go to the gym by ourselves, we go home, and we repeat. And that self-reliance is glorified, which is scary to me.'

With this in mind, Jillian started The Joy List, where she promotes events that facilitate moments of deeper connection. The events are similar in concept to the old-style literary 'salons' where people would connect through exchange of stories and ideas. This concept is enjoying a revival across the world as many push back against the ironic lack of true connection in the digital age. In addition, Jillian hosts a Joy List Social once a month. When people check in, they are then introduced to another attendee and are given a conversation prompt, such as, 'What has brought you joy this week?' (Rather than having to use the awkward networking trope, 'So, what do you do?')

I am currently working with a client to bring this concept into the workplace to support belonging and inclusion. 'Curiosity Camps' will become a part of their programme, replacing the traditional approach to D&I programmes, which usually roll out a series of compulsory workshops and training sessions. The idea of the camps is to promote belonging and inclusion through curiosity, stories and sharing of ideas. Workshops and training programmes essentially instruct people to think in a certain way. We know that human behaviour doesn't work like that – just as we can't make somebody understand us by repeatedly screaming 'understand me!' at them – so, why do we keep doing it? I would be willing to bet that every single person reading this book has watched a TED Talk. I would also bet that the majority have watched one TED Talk, been curious about another that is listed, so watched a further talk. And you will have learned something from each one, or it may have changed your perspective on something. TED Talks spark intellectual curiosity and leave us with questions such as 'What if . . . ?' The amazing thing is that nobody told you that you had to do this. Human beings are curious creatures and we seek out stories or theories or insights told well (often with a dose of humour). It is why we read, watch television, go to the theatre, watch documentaries and repeat interesting things we have learned to others.

The Curiosity Camp philosophy is thus:

- People learn to understand one another on a deeper level through stories. They tap into shared human emotions, which bridges the divide with people who are different from us by evoking empathy.

- Curiosity has to be self-directed. You can't direct someone else's journey – that is like giving somebody a directed route through a maze, which makes the whole thing seem a pointless pursuit.
- Conversation, debate and sharing of ideas, when there is nothing at stake, helps people to connect on a deeper level. This is different from the conversations that happen around work when the dynamics are complex.
- Connecting within or to such events gives people a moment in time when they are fully present and such mindfulness is one of the most powerful ways to protect well-being.

Organisations can provide a variety of low-cost, interesting and thought-provoking experiences to drive connectivity, belonging and well-being. There is no limit to how creative you can get in this context and offering choice not only empowers, but also caters to the needs of different personality styles. I often cringe now when I look back at times I have used activities in workshops or conferences that can only be described as 'forced friend-making' and must have been so difficult for those who were more introverted or socially anxious. (If any of you happen to be reading this, I am truly sorry that younger me put you through this. Lesson learnt.)

It is important that there is a consistent flow of activities so that the journey towards individual understanding is sustained and so that a true belonging culture can emerge. You have to accept that there are some who will not want to engage or take part, but don't think that these people would have engaged any more in compulsory workshops. As this approach becomes weaved into the fabric of the organisation, strong cultures have a way of making people evolve or self-select out – which isn't necessarily a bad thing.

Here are three examples of the sorts of activities that could be included in the Curiosity Camp approach:

- *Curiosity Camp events:* these conform to the traditional salon approach with up to 10 people coming together, hosted by an internal or external 'expert', physically or virtually, to discuss and debate an idea. They can start with a question around which the debate can evolve and then a position or idea shared by the host. I recently held such a session with a global senior talent team and started by showing a two-minute video, which posed questions around 'What is a community?' Once complete, I told the group that I don't believe that traditional organisations are communities and that this is a structural issue due to the role of the HR function. Deliberately being contentious or adopting an extreme or novel perspective (within reason!) is a great way of opening up debate. I have also co-hosted sessions where the other host takes the opposite perspective – this is particularly useful for virtual events where it often takes a little longer for people to warm up and join the conversation.

- *Sofa sessions:* these are more like the TED Talk concept, with a larger virtual audience gathering to listen to a presenter share a story or idea. These are between 10–15 minutes long, designed to fit a coffee break and recorded to be accessed on the intranet later. Again, a diverse range of presenters can be included, from external experts or those internally who have a particular expertise, interest or story to tell.
- *Lightening moments:* these are short videos (1–2 minutes long) that are distributed by email and present an idea, provoke thinking or tell a story.

When planning events, you can weave in repeated themes that spark curiosity, promote understanding and are representative of a diverse range of people.

part 3

How to embed the culture of belonging

chapter 8

Keep the change going

Building in measures before, during and after implementation of your Belonging Plan is critical for progress and evolution. Once you have implemented your original Belonging Plan, the challenge is to create the momentum that means employees *experience* and *feel* a sense of community and belonging. Development of a community is not a destination; communities evolve, shape-shift, react to external forces, continually strengthen internal forces and direction is guided by the people within it. This chapter will help you to do this and cover:

- how to be clear on what you are measuring and why
- developing a dashboard fit for your plan and your organisation
- how a sense of community develops over time and how to measure where you are in the journey
- how organisations with a belonging culture can support employees when they leave the community

Measuring what matters

There is no shortage of information out there on how to measure D&I progress, but the majority of the guidance is directed towards traditional approaches, is managed by spreadsheet and designed for the main purpose of reporting success to the executive team. I am not going to go through these measures as there is little value to add to the information that exists. Measurement based on developing a belonging culture has a range of variables, each of which has a specific purpose and it is important that you are clear on why you are measuring them.

Metrics identified in the plan

The Belonging Plan you developed included data and employee experience metrics against each of the identified themes, so this is the obvious place to start. Continual monitoring of these metrics is important not just because you are able to monitor progress, but they are also the basis upon which you might evolve the plan. As discussed already, the plan is a guide and may change as progress is made. More appropriate metrics may be identified, progress may be quicker or slower than predicted or additional metrics may be added to give greater insight. In addition, as progress is made and goals are reached, these are the metrics that will help you to think about 'what next?', as well as consider what you have learned through the initial implementation.

Measuring and reporting against the value proposition for stakeholders

If you want the executive team to keep topping up your budget and stakeholders to remain on side, being clear on how you have delivered against the value proposition is key. This is about showing the decision makers how activity has supported and delivered against business priorities. But there is also another opportunity here. When you are reporting progress to the decision-making team, keep in mind the process you went through when you were presenting the business case. It is important to keep the team emotionally engaged and to keep telling them the next part of the narrative. Your focus then was 'Not on my watch' and this is the emotion you must keep tapping into – showing them that, under their watch, things are changing and improving. Relating employee stories about well-being and belonging, alongside data, keeps both hearts and minds connected to the initiative. This continuing commitment from the top is critical to the strengthening of a belonging culture.

Essential reporting metrics

There are some measures that are non-negotiable from a compliance perspective and, depending on the size and maturity of the organisation, you will, more than likely, already have the systems in place to record these metrics.

- Different geographies will have different legislative requirements, which, for global organisations, means having awareness of what these are in each location.
- Professional and industry bodies increasingly have D&I standards to which member organisations are expected to adhere.
- D&I is becoming a critical factor in investor attraction and relations. Investors are increasingly looking for organisations who align with their own values and recognise the need for strong D&I policies that attract and retain top talent.

Measuring culture change

This is where metrics for measuring a sense of belonging veer away from traditional D&I measurement. It is the only way you will, first, know whether you are making a difference and, second, know how to keep evolving your approach. However, it is not easy and nor is it an exact science – as Kirsty Bashforth says in her book *Culture Shift*, it is about 'filling buckets, not spreadsheets'.

Researchers, management consultancies and organisational development professionals have been debating and redefining best practice for measuring organisational culture since the concept was first introduced in the 1950s. Yet, there is still little agreement on what best practice is. So, what is the problem with this culture thing and why is it still so hotly debated? Well, first, there is no one agreed definition about what it is – even after all this time. Leaders talk of developing a strong culture or changing the culture without really stopping to think about what it is they mean or even why it is important. There was a collective leadership sigh of relief when big data came onto the scene as there was finally something concrete that could be applied to the enigma of culture (or, as the academic Andrew Pettigrew describes it, 'a riddle wrapped in a mystery wrapped in an enigma'). The emergence of big data certainly has been a huge help for larger organisations where the exercise previously seemed an impossible feat and, even for smaller organisations, greater awareness of data analysis has meant more scope for personalising the approach. But it still hasn't solved the problem. To give you an idea of the extent of the spectrum of approaches, a 2020 academic review of tools for measuring organisational culture listed a total of 82 different instruments. Not only are each of these, at best, marginally successful, but research has also shown that inappropriate use of such instruments can actually disadvantage organisations.

The issue lies in the age-old problem of organisations and leaders wanting certainty. They want to manage everything. So, they want to measure everything. Then, they feel that they are able to control everything, turning the dials up or down according to need. When an issue arises that is difficult to define or resolve, culture is normally put to blame. Hence the desire for (and the poor deployment of) instruments like the 82 available to them. But this thinking is unhelpful given the two critical variables in the conundrum, which are anything but stable and predictable – people and the external environment. In a volatile and unpredictable world, organisations need to start taking a more flexible and emergent approach to culture.

In developing a belonging culture, the ultimate goal is clear – where everyone is included, everyone will thrive. In this book, I have described the principles that underpin a belonging culture and how they essentially form an interdependent ecosystem. The approach has to be flexible and emergent in order to respond according to needs, while the goal is always to ensure there is a strong sense of belonging and, if there isn't, to understand where in the ecosystem the problem may lie. Equally, when there is an increasing sense of belonging in the organisation, examination of how this has emerged can help direct future activity.

Measuring a belonging culture

- The Belonging Audit is your starting point and this should be your annual standard for measuring progress. You may want to consider whether this replaces your annual engagement survey, if you currently have one, or whether you want to run them both in parallel. Consideration should be given as to the purpose of the engagement survey over and above that of the belonging survey. Running both has the potential for diluting the perceived commitment to belonging and runs the risk of survey fatigue, as well as data overload.
- After the first year, progress should be aligned to impact on the performance metrics described earlier such as:
  - performance data
  - retention data
  - absence data
  - well-being data.

- In addition, regular or, where possible, continuous tracking of performance data can allow ongoing tweaking of plans according to need.
- Observational and anecdotal data provide richness and insight when measuring belonging. Using a system for the team to record these and then looking for patterns by either tagging each piece of data or using a word cloud can provide valuable insight to the felt experience of belonging.
- Get creative with how you can collect more qualitative data. For example, put in a system where each day team members are randomly assigned an employee to reach out to for a two-minute chat or to ask a question about belonging. Employees should be made aware of such initiatives in advance, as well as the anonymous nature of any data captured in the conversation.
- Pulse surveys to check in throughout the year can be useful but it is, perhaps, more useful to have a weekly belonging question. This can be emailed or even texted to employees, making it easy for them to answer immediately. The results can be reported weekly, keeping commitment to belonging front of mind across the organisation.
- All of the above measures must be considered alongside a record of activity so that regular analysis can help you to understand what is really making a difference and why. This can help to make the right adjustments to what you do next and how you build future plans.

Measuring *your* way

When it comes to measuring and reporting, there are no hard and fast rules – only that it has to work for your organisation. This will depend on the size, geography and maturity of the organisation, as well as any standard reporting procedures across the business. In larger organisations, real-time data analytics provide the ability to get a clear picture of what is happening in the organisation today, whereas, in smaller organisations, frequent analysis, intuition and clearer line of sight can be just as successful in providing insights and informing direction. The main thing is to measure what will help you and don't get into analysis paralysis. Keep it as simple as possible and focused on your defined goals.

Larger organisations deploy dashboard software for traditional D&I reporting. This software provides visual displays of metrics and progress, using real-time analytics that can be drilled up or down for granular or big-picture detail. There are many providers, including opensource platforms such as Google Dashboard, which provides options for smaller organisations.

While useful for analysis and reporting, dashboards are highly quantitative in nature, reflecting the traditional approach to D&I measurement. Reporting and measuring belonging requires the input of qualitative data, reflecting the human experience of belonging that cannot be represented in numbers. So, when developing any measurement and reporting mechanisms, include data such as results from weekly belonging surveys or patterns in observational data. Bring the human element into reporting to bring substance to hard data.

Developing a sense of community

With the best will in the world, no plan will ever allow you to develop a sense of community overnight. All communities develop differently, depending on context, purpose, the individuals, climate and the nature of their interactions. The ultimate aim of developing a community is self-determination – the community itself directs its evolution over time. While there is a wealth of research into community in other concepts, the workplace has been largely neglected other than consideration of developing communities of practice within organisations to drive inter-team collaboration. Based on established community development theory and considering the principles of the belonging model, the organisation-community development will evolve through four phases, outlined in the following table.

Development phase	Theme
Inception: the plan is implemented	Awareness: the whole organisation is aware of the belonging focus and plan
Disruption: leaders transition to facilitative role	Leadership change: leaders adapt at differing rates with some resistance from those who prefer a 'top down' approach. At the same time, employees start to experience a sense of having their needs met by the community
Participation: employees influence and contribute	Empowerment: following leadership transition, employees feel able to both influence and contribute to decision making in the community
Community: employees are emotionally connected	Citizenship: an established sense of agency, purpose and ownership creates deeper connections between the employee and the organisation

The rate at which development occurs is unknown and is dependent on a number of often unpredictable, uncontrollable variables, as outlined above. However, being aware of where you are in the development of a community can help you to understand where you may be 'stuck', analyse why this may be the case and redefine plans accordingly.

A sense of community comes from a feeling of collective experience, so, determining how strong it is requires understanding of how it is felt at an individual level. A validated and established framework for a sense of community, upon which the development timeline above is based, describes these felt experiences in four dimensions (according to McMillan and Chavis, 1996)[1]:

- *Needs fulfilment:* members feel their needs are met by the community.
- *Group membership:* a feeling of belonging and interpersonal connectivity.
- *Influence:* a sense of value and the ability to make a difference.
- *Emotional connectivity:* stronger attachments based on shared experiences and mutual concern for well-being.

A brief questionnaire based on these dimensions can be adapted to use within organisations. Using these measures will help to give a high-level indication of where you are in the journey in terms of community development and can be used annually after you have implemented your plan. In addition, it is useful to understand at which point in their tenure employees feel they become a part of the community by having new starters complete the questionnaire when they join, at 6 months and 12 months. This gives another data point to assess the strength of the community.

Brief Sense of Community Scale[2]

Questions	Strongly agree	Agree	Neither agree/ disagree	Disagree	Strongly disagree
I can get what I need in this organisation					
This organisation helps me fulfil my needs					
I feel like a member of this organisation					

▶

Questions	Strongly agree	Agree	Neither agree/ disagree	Disagree	Strongly disagree
I belong in this organisation					
I have a say about what goes on in my organisation					
People in this organisation are good at influencing each other					
I feel connected to this organisation					
I have a good bond with others in this organisation					

Source: Adapted from the Brief Sense of Community scale, developed by Peterson, Speer and McMillan (2008)

Expanding the community

'An enterprise is a living and active part of the community. They need each other to be able to prosper, and often to survive.'

Andrea Rasca, founder and chief executive of Mercato Metropolitano

The power of a sense of community can be extended to external communities, strengthening a sense of belonging to employees within. A sense of pride about the organisation, and applying its strengths to create value in other communities, is becoming a prominent feature in what younger generations are looking for in employers. They want organisations that live their values and make a positive difference to the world. They want to get involved in things that don't just pay the bills, but create value where value is needed the most. They care about what they can achieve outside of organisational goals and expect employers to support them in doing so. In a 2017 survey by Deloitte, 89 per cent of employees said that organisations who support employee volunteering provide a better working environment than those that don't.[3] The same survey also found that such support boosts morale and brand perception. Yet another survey by the

Telegraph newspaper in the UK found that just 22 per cent of employers thought that local community or charity support was a priority for employees.[4] Organisations are missing a trick, as this has become more fundamental than the previous nod at corporate social responsibility inferred – or, indeed, achieved.

Strong communities recognise the ecosystem of other communities within which they exist and overlap. They recognise the responsibilities that exist within this context and the value of helping other communities to flourish. In an organisational context, this might include:

- *Local communities:* partnering with the local community brings a wealth of benefits for both parties. Organisations can lend expertise, skills or resources to support the needs of the local community. They may lend meeting space or host local events, for example, which bring the two communities closer together. My own organisation works in partnership with the local town council to drive inclusion and belonging in the area, as well as provide training for local businesses. The UK organisation Timpson recruits those who have served time in prison to help cut reoffending rates. There is no limit or one-size-fits-all – it starts with the question, 'What can we do to create value?' As many employees also live in the local community, understanding and supporting these needs means that the organisation is creating value for their employees outside of the parameters of the organisation.
- *Local education providers:* partnership between education providers and local businesses provides a wealth of benefits for business, the local community and society as a whole. Some organisations sponsor schools or donate equipment, but, outside of providing direct financial support, the scope is limitless. The UK organisation Business in the Community provides guidance and resources for organisations to partner with local education providers to benefit the most disadvantaged school leavers as well as provide curriculum support to drive innovation and bridge the gap between education and work. Work experience schemes and graduate recruitment can ensure that opportunities are maximised for marginalised groups in the community. Just think of the skills and knowledge that exist within your organisation and how this could benefit the lives of young people in the community.
- *Local charities:* organisations can choose to support one particular charity or else allow employees to choose their own charity to volunteer within. Many organisations partner with charities that will benefit most from the nature of their work, but the very nature of business means that all organisations have expertise that will benefit the running of charities. Many larger charities are aware of how they want to partner with organisations but local, smaller

charities are more likely to benefit most from support. Consider things such as training programmes: you could provide or invite charity workers along to training you are running internally, such as leadership programmes or sales training, work experience opportunities or even short-term 'job swaps'. Think about charities that support disadvantaged people and how you may be able to offer jobs, placements or work experience. My organisation provides neurodiversity training for managers and employees at a local charity, which allows them to recruit and provide appropriate support for neurodivergent employees. Again, the opportunities are limitless and, simply by supporting employees in volunteering, you will find your employees find their own ways to help.

The changing community

'All change is loss, and all loss must be mourned.'

Harry Levinson, psychologist

Throughout our life we join and leave many communities. Sometimes we are only a part of the community briefly, sometimes for life. Sometimes the experience is positive and sometimes it isn't. Sometimes we choose to leave a community and sometimes we have no choice. The same goes for careers; throughout our lives most of us will be a part of several organisations and some only one. Whichever way, leaving, at some point, is inevitable and, for whatever reason that may be, it is often experienced as a loss. Organisations with a focus on belonging must think about the legacy that remains when an employee leaves and provide support as far as possible to protect well-being.

When people must leave: dismissal

It goes without saying that any process that leads to dismissal should both be fair and comply with the law. However, organisations frequently fail to separate the process from the person and, other than communicating what support the employee is entitled to, take few measures to protect their well-being. Regardless of the circumstances leading to the dismissal, the process and outcome are bound to have an emotional impact, to a greater or lesser degree. In addition, the experience is a major life event, with potentially far-reaching and devastating consequences. The employee who is being dismissed is also a partner, a parent, a child or a sibling and the emotional impact goes beyond just the employee's individual experience. Organisations should lessen the impact as much as possible by providing resources that can help through the transition, such as financial advice or CV writing, as well as offering independent support throughout the process, such as a well-being helpline or coach.

When people decide to leave: resignation

Resigning from a job is emotionally difficult. Even if it is leaving an organisation where you are unhappy to go to another job, the act signals a conscious decision for change and, even when the experience hasn't been positive, there is still a period of reflection, perhaps sadness, that occurs with any sense of an ending. Leaving a job you have loved or an organisation where you have truly felt part of a community to pursue another opportunity can be a very difficult decision to make and can cause a lot of apprehension. Of course, the first instinct a leader has when somebody resigns is to ask why, which is of course important, but how the employee responds may ignite an emotional response from the leader. As part of leadership development in a belonging culture, leaders should learn to accept resignations graciously, to acknowledge the emotional difficulty of the decision and to express gratitude for the employee having been a part of the community. How resignation is handled can make a significant difference to the legacy the organisation leaves with an employee. Such an approach is also appreciated by those left behind, if the employee has been a popular or influential figure in the organisation.

When community membership ends: retirement

Retirement can be a bittersweet experience for employees and is a significant life event. Probably more so than any other way of leaving an organisation, there may be apprehension, sadness and a profound sense of an ending. The potential for mental health problems and loneliness after retirement is significant and, given the ageing demographic of today's workforce, many organisations now offer at-retirement support. However, Employee Benefits/Wealth at Work Pensions research in 2019 demonstrated that the motivation for organisations providing this support is driven mainly by duty of care and as part of employee branding, rather than concern for ensuring a smooth transition out of the workplace.[5] Unfortunately, when organisations provide support because 'they think they should', it often doesn't achieve what it is intended to.

Retirement support should start well in advance of the event itself to allow the employee to make decisions about their future and have time to transition emotionally. Providing a coach can help in this respect, and additional support might also be provided to help with the transition, such as financial planning or helping to find opportunities for volunteering. The main focus should be showing the employee that they have value in the next phase of life just as they have during their career. As with resignation, the organisation should express their gratitude to the employee for them having been a valuable part of their community. After retirement, the organisation should check in with the employee after the first few weeks to ensure the transition has not had a significant impact on well-being.

When major disruption happens: redundancy

Redundancies are always difficult but, sadly, inevitable, particularly in a volatile environment like we live in today. Regardless of circumstances, the announcement is often a shock to employees, the period leading up to redundancy stressful and employees leaving is emotionally difficult not just for those who are departing, but also for those remaining who often suffer with 'survivor's guilt'. The impact on well-being should not be under-estimated by organisations. The process often feels clinical, despite adherence to best practice and the provision of things such as outplacement support. While there are some who may welcome the redundancy, the majority don't and it has a significant impact on their lives beyond the organisation. Organisations with a belonging culture need to ensure that they show employees that they care about them as individuals, that they will provide support for their well-being, however they can. And, more than that, when the process is over, rather than closing the door behind the departees and breathing a sigh of relief, organisations should communicate to employees that they are sad that this has happened but they are grateful that the employee has been a part of their community. Redundancy is definitely a prime example of a situation in which organisations with a culture of belonging must put humanity at the heart.

Notes

1 McMillan, D.W. and Chavis, D.M. (1986) 'Sense of community: A definition and theory', *Journal of Community Psychology*, 14, 6–23.

2 Peterson, N.A., Speer, P. and McMillan, D.W. (2008) 'Validation of a brief sense of community scale: confirmation of the principle theory of sense of community.' *Journal of Community Psychology*, 36, 61–73.

3 '2017 Deloitte Volunteerism Survey', June, based on 1,000 US adults aged 18+, employed full- or part-time, who have volunteered in the past 12 months. Available at: https://www2.deloitte.com/content/dam/Deloitte/us/Documents/about-deloitte/us-2017-deloitte-volunteerism-survey.pdf

4 Coleman, A. (2019) 'How can businesses support local communities?', *The Telegraph*, 21 August.

5 The survey – available at: https://employeebenefits.co.uk/employee-benefits-pensions-2019/ – was conducted in October 2019 among readers of https://employeebenefits.co.uk and received 135 responses. Respondents are involved in pension strategy at their organisation, either as a primary decision maker or decision influencer.

chapter 9

It's down to you

Every one of us has a role and a responsibility in driving social change, not just in the workplace, but in our communities and society in general. We have a choice: we can look on from the side lines and shake our heads disapprovingly at the actions of others that negatively impact belonging; or we can step in and commit to being part of a movement that will create a change in society that is well overdue. This chapter will include:

- why and how belonging must start with self-care and self-compassion
- why and how we must all take responsibility for driving social change
- why we can and should be optimistic about the future

This book has focused on belonging and well-being in the workplace, but the principles are no less relevant in wider society and never more so than now.

- A 2018 survey by *The Economist* found that 22 per cent of adults in the USA and 23 per cent in the UK said that they often or always feel lonely – figures that increased exponentially with the onset of the pandemic.
- Worldwide, the World Health Organization reports that suicide is the leading cause of death in 15–29-year-olds and 20 per cent of children and adolescents have a mental health condition.
- In 2020, Ipsos reported that 78 per cent of people believe we live in an increasingly dangerous world, while 52 per cent believe there will be global conflict within the next 25 years.

Start with you: self-care and self-compassion

'The truth is: belonging starts with self-acceptance. Your level of
belonging, in fact, can never be greater than your level of self-acceptance, because believing that you're enough is what gives you the courage to be authentic, vulnerable and imperfect.'

Brené Brown, researcher, author, professor

Before you can create a sense of belonging for anyone else or contribute to
change that will make a difference for others, you have to start with yourself.
Before you start rolling your eyes and muttering about psychobabble or spirit-
uality nonsense, hear me out.

We all have aspects of ourselves, to greater or lesser degrees, that we find
difficult to accept and will tend to push away or hide. In doing so, we signal
that these things do not 'belong'. If we don't ignore them, then we might go on a
never-ending quest for self-improvement, lining our bookshelves with self-help
books and signing up for courses we never complete. All this serves to do is compound the feeling of 'not good enough', which is detrimental to well-being and
mental health, thereby impacting your resilience. Seems illogical, right? As long
as we act as though we cannot accept all of who we are, we will never feel a true
sense of belonging anywhere – and, given that it impacts our ability to extend
empathy to others, we may negatively affect a sense of belonging for others.

Get to know – and challenge – your core beliefs

The thing about the core beliefs we hold about ourselves is that we are always
subconsciously looking for evidence to prove that they are right, which affects
the ability to be objective in our judgements. If these core beliefs have been
developed in reaction to automatic negative thoughts, they will impact your self-
worth. And, if you feel unworthy, you will look out for signs that others do too,
thereby impacting your ability to feel a sense of belonging.

Identifying your core beliefs

Look for patterns and themes in your thinking:

• What negative thoughts do you frequently have about yourself? What does
  your inner critic say about you?

- Think back to recent negative experiences or situations. How did you interpret them? Did the same negative thoughts occur?
- Now imagine you are somebody else responding objectively to the inner critic. Are the interpretations of negative experiences fair? How could they be reframed?

This exercise must be practised regularly and the key is to recognise when the inner critic pops up. Acknowledge it, but don't get caught up in an internal dialogue. Instead, consider how you can reframe your thinking as per the exercise.

Know thyself

I have talked a lot about the power of being curious in this book, and being curious about yourself is no less powerful. Knowing, accepting and being comfortable with who you are is not only fundamental to good mental health, but it allows your identity to remain stable across a range of contexts, rather than feeling you must adapt to be like those around you. Without self-acceptance, it is impossible to be authentic. In addition, as Maya Angelou said, 'When we know better, we do better.' When we have greater awareness of why we behave in certain ways, we exercise greater control over our actions.

How to be curious about yourself:

- Ask questions in a curious way. If something goes wrong, don't think 'What is wrong with me? I am useless', think 'Why did that happen? What did I do?' Being curious allows you to explore objectively and uncovers things about yourself that you may not have understood before.
- Accept the faults you find because they are a part of you. Don't set about trying to change them, just as you wouldn't suggest that a friend should do so – we tend to accept the faults of others better than our own. Accept them and think curiously about how you can get over some of the challenges they present.
- Look for strengths too. It may sound obvious, but, depending on your personality, you will be more apt to look for either strengths or faults. If you are finding only one or the other, ask why? What is it you're not seeing? And, when you find your strengths, be amazed by them, learn to be grateful for them, rather than lamenting your faults.
- Set boundaries for negative emotions. Shame, guilt and judgement are enemies of self-curiosity, stopping us from truly knowing ourselves and flooding our emotions disproportionately. These emotions have a truly detrimental effect on mental well-being if they are sustained over a long period of time. When they pop up, acknowledge them and turn your attention towards positive actions.

Practise self-care

I don't mean light a candle and listen to whale songs (though, if this is your sort of thing, go ahead!). Self-care is an holistic, multi-dimensional approach to protecting well-being. It means investing time in physical, mental, emotional and psychological care. There is a wealth of resources available for developing self-care plans and leaders are increasingly realising how critical it is for performance. It takes a while to understand what your individual well-being needs are but, once you know what they are, you are able to monitor and adjust accordingly, which is particularly important in times of stress.

Make it a priority and a habit.

Understanding your well-being needs

Use the template below to monitor and understand your personal needs so you can create a self-care plan. Complete it at the end of the day for a couple of weeks to see what aspects impact your mood and energy the most.

How am I feeling today?	
How is my mood? (On a scale of 1 poor, 10 excellent)	1 2 3 4 5 6 7 8 9 10
Describe what emotions I have	
How are my energy levels? (On a scale of 1 poor, 10 excellent)	1 2 3 4 5 6 7 8 9 10
Do I have any physical symptoms today?	
Physical	
What time do I go to bed and wake up?	
How many hours sleep did I get?	
How much water have I had?	
Have I had any exercise?	
What have I eaten today?	
Have I had any alcohol today?	

Psychological	
How many hours did I work today?	
Have I felt stressed, anxious or depressed?	
Have I engaged in a hobby or something I really like to do?	
Have I made time to relax?	
Have I been out into the fresh air?	
Emotional	
Have I connected with family/friends?	
Have I spoken to anybody about how I feel?	
What three good things have happened today?	
What is the strongest emotion I have felt during the day and why?	
Have I laughed today?	

The future of belonging

'(Social change is) change that makes society or workplaces more humanizing, in terms of fostering human rights, and thriving towards what would seem more just, ecologically sustainable, inclusive, empowering and peaceful.'

Hany Shoukry, 'Coaching for Social Change' (2017)[1]

I would like to end this journey on a positive note because, although there is much to fear and lament in the world right now, it is not all doom and gloom. The turbulence of the past few years and the polarisation that has plagued societies that are trying to make sense of it is also making people hungry for change. I see chinks of light in many places now and it is important that we all go looking for them so that we too can be a part of the change.

Be a part of the change

Social change happens from the ground up and, if enough people choose to opt out of the dualism that has increasingly plagued society for the last few years, we can start to make it happen. Research by the journal *ScienceDaily* in 2018 found that it takes only 25 per cent of any group to stand up for change in order to create an inflection point.[2] Imagine the change if your organisation could get 25 per cent of employees to commit to creating a sense of belonging for all. Imagine if communities and societies did the same.

Here are some simple ideas that will help you to be a part of the change in your own small way:

- Recognise the impact of the echo chambers created by targeted media and expand your information sources.
- Ask questions and seek to understand those who are different from you. Get used to feeling uncomfortable.
- Don't pre-judge. Different doesn't have to mean bad.
- If you use social media, do so positively to drive change – don't allow yourself to be dragged into the toxic binary thinking that exists online.
- Live by the South African proverb that says: 'If you want to go fast, go alone. If you want to go far, go together.' Work positively with people to create change rather than fight against those who resist it. Remember, it only takes 25 per cent.

Future evolution of the workplace

The German sociologist Max Weber had a lot to answer for when he proposed his theory of bureaucracy in the early 20th century. It was his belief that bureaucracy is necessary to maximise efficiency, maintain order and reduce favouritism. In addition, he believed that power and hierarchy are pre-requisite to this command-and-control approach. Throughout the 20th century and early 21st century, through the technological and information ages, this approach dominated. For the past decade, we have started to see a slow shift in workplace culture. Driven by Millennials and an increasing number of start-ups, the emerging themes have been agility, flexibility, innovation and purpose. Prior to 2020, so much had been written about these themes and how they can be embedded in larger organisations, but, in the shackles of industrial-age command and control, bringing with it layers of crippling bureaucracy, little progress was made. In a *Forbes* article, Brian Bi, former software engineer at Google, writes of how he believes we are transitioning from the Age of Information to the Age of Reckoning:

> **'I believe that in order to confront the major problems that we will face this century, we are going to have to look inward and confront some uncomfortable truths about human nature, understand the fact that technology can amplify both the best and the worst aspects of it, and possibly come together to make big sacrifices in order to build a world that's truly better for all of us. This is the "reckoning" that I speak of.'**

Then 2020 happened and so did the beginning of real change in the workplace, as breaking from the shackles became necessity and it really did appear to be the dawn of the Age of Reckoning.

Where does it go from here?

While the legacy of the pandemic remains yet to be seen, there are indications of likely changes in the future that mirror start-up thinking and look to dismantle Weber's bureaucratic approach:

- *Remote-hybrid working:* according to a 2020 Gartner survey of 317 CFOs and finance leaders on 30 March, 2020,[3] 74 per cent of organisations plan to shift some of their employees to a remote working model indefinitely. In May 2020, Twitter told all its employees they could work from home indefinitely. As the cost, well-being and environmental benefits are realised, remote and hybrid working look set to become the norm as the future evolves.
- *Office space:* this, of course, means that there will be less need for physical office space and organisations are thinking about what this means for the future. While some are already giving up or selling off office spaces, others are considering how office spaces can be redesigned to be less formal and collaborative. In addition, it is predicted that more organisations will move towards use of shared working spaces, such as WeWork, realising the cost benefits of having flexible hubs throughout the country, as well as the increased potential for talent attraction, given the increased geography.
- *Technology for agility:* the 2020 crisis gave technology the moment we had all been waiting for when business-critical agility became the focus for organisations. Many business models are adapting in the wake of this to serve the needs of increased digital first customers as well as collaborative tools that support remote working. Having experienced the fast deployment of new technologies, many organisations are now considering more rapidly advancing technologies, such as artificial intelligence (AI), machine learning, deep learning and advanced robotics, all of which support agility and the drive for innovation.

- *Stripped-out bureaucracy:* in their book *Humanocracy: Creating Organizations as Amazing as the People Inside Them*, Gary Hamel and Michele Zanini rally against Weber-esque bureaucracy, presenting a blueprint for how organisations can become 'resilient and daring' by stripping out the bureaucracy holding back progress and agility. As organisations rapidly adapted in response to the pandemic, we saw this in action. There was no room – or indeed need – for unnecessary procedures, processes or administration as employees went about creating the unknown. Today, we are seeing leaders reconceiving organisations, moving away from bureaucracy and towards those that are continually shape shifting. Alibaba has developed what it calls the 'self-tuning enterprise', where algorithmic learning is applied throughout the organisation, and Zappos have given all teams the autonomy to create their own value propositions, as well as make their own investment decisions.

- *Decreased hierarchy:* in line with the benefits of stripping out bureaucracy, leaders are starting to realise the engagement and agility benefits of breaking down hierarchical barriers. Decisions can be made and implemented more quickly if they are devolved from senior leadership. Involving and empowering all layers in the development of strategy and innovations brings together more diverse perspectives and the dismantling of power gives way to less political, more collaborative cultures.

- *Increased focus on social purpose:* as well as being a priority of younger generations, as discussed in this book, many organisations are starting to feel and act on their responsibility to contribute to solving the most pressing social and environmental problems we face today. In the USA, the Business Roundtable, which brings together CEOs from some of the largest organisations, brought its members together to make a commitment to social change. Many organisations are looking to improve and socialise their social responsibility by being assessed and certified by B Corp, meaning they 'are legally required to consider the impact of their decisions on their workers, customers, suppliers, community, and the environment'. Start-ups, too, are more likely to begin building their businesses based on the ethos 'Do well to do good'.

If the world of work continues to move in this direction, the evolution of the organisation as a community, with an increased sense of belonging for all, will flourish. These changes may also account for the results of research at the end of 2020 by the ADP Research Institute. It reported that 84 per cent of employees today are feeling optimistic about the next five years in the workplace, just a 2 per cent drop from pre-pandemic levels and, despite the uncertainty, 75 per cent said they felt buoyant about the year ahead. I am heartened by these figures – after all, hope floats.

And finally . . .

The belonging movement is gathering pace. In all aspects of society, we are starting to see the shift. The Othering and Belonging Institute, part of UC Berkeley in the USA, brings together academics, researchers, stakeholders, communicators and policy makers. It describes itself as:

'. . . a diverse and vibrant hub generating work centered on realizing a world where all people belong, where belonging entails being respected at a level that includes the right to both contribute and make demands upon society and political and cultural institutions.'

Along with their European initiative 'Toward Belonging', the institute is bringing together the strands of activity from a range of institutions that will generate the momentum needed to create true social change.

Your organisation can be a part of the change. You can be a part of the change. We can make a difference, so let's do this together. Let's be part of the 25 per cent.

Notes

1 Shoukry, H. (2017) 'Coaching for social change', in T. Bachkirova, G. Spence and D. Drake (eds) *The SAGE Handbook of Coaching* (pp. 176–191). Sage Publications inc.

2 University of Pennsylvania (2018) 'Tipping point for large-scale social change', 7 June. Available at: https://www.sciencedaily.com/releases/2018/06/180607141009.htm

3 Available at: https://www.gartner.com/en/newsroom/press-releases/2020-04-03-gartner-cfo-surey-reveals-74-percent-of-organizations-to-shift-some-employees-to-remote-work-permanently2

Index

ability, as determinant of privilege and disadvantage 9
absenteeism 64
Accenture 20, 23–4
acceptance 37
accessibility 112
accountability 104
Adler, Alfred 21
ADP Research Institute 172
advocacy 106
Age of Reckoning 171
agency 36, 76–8, 82–3, 114
aggression 77
Alibaba 172
allyship 118–20
Amazon 145
American Psychological Association 126
amygdala hijack 125
Angelou, Maya 167
anonymity 55, 56, 134, 155
anti-racism 141–3
anxiety 22, 128, 134
assessment centres 78
attention deficit hyperactivity disorder (ADHD) 112, 118, 138–9
audience 94–6, 98–9
audit *see* Belonging Audit

B Corp 172
banter 77
Bashforth, Kirsty 109, 153

Beard, Mary 78
behaviour frameworks 78–9, 124
beliefs, knowing and challenging your core 166–9
belonging xvii, 3, 6, 13, 21–7, 31, 169–72
Belonging Audit 53, 110, 154
    before you begin 53–4
    doing 55–61
    planning 54–5
    questionnaire 56–60
    reviewing 61–5
belonging culture 33–8, 75–6, 103, 152, 154–5
Belonging Plan
    building your 67–91
    commitment to 103–4
    implementation 107–30
    keeping the change going 151–62
    metrics 152
    pitch presentation 103
    stakeholders 105
    value proposition 96, 98
Bi, Brian 170–1
big data 153
Black Lives Matter 142
blame cultures 80, 81
blind recruitment 113
bonus system 124
Brandwatch 74–5, 128–9
Breivik, Anders 5
Brief Sense of Community Scale 157–8

Brown, Brené 166
Buffer 137
bullying 19, 77
bureaucracy 80, 145, 170, 171, 172
business case 94–6
Business in the Community 159
Business Roundtable 172
buy-in *see* organisational buy-in
bystanders 120, 140

'calling it out' 16, 18, 34, 44, 45, 140–1
career progression 64, 115–18, 121
carer status 10
charity support 158–60
Churchill, Winston 4
code-switching xxii
collaboration, and open-mindedness 37
collective consciousness 48–9, 88
command-and-control approach 81, 170
communism 5
communities, organisations and teams as
          31–2, 49–50, 72–5, 114, 156–62
community xix–xx
community charter 127–8
community managers 128–9
compassion 46
competence frameworks 123–4
confidantes 120
confidentiality 122, 132–4
connected teams 46–9, 87–9
connectivity 34, 37, 38, 75, 76, 84–5, 135–6,
          144–8
consciousness, collective 48–9, 88
consistency, belonging culture 33, 75, 76
control, and disempowerment 77
conversation, connecting through 145–8
core beliefs, knowing and challenging your
          166–9
corporate social responsibility 159
courage, and leadership 44–5, 86, 87, 140
cover letters 78
covering up of exclusion 16–17
COVID-19 pandemic 4, 12, 32, 80, 135, 165,
          171, 172
criminal convictions 112, 159
cultural awareness training 118

cultural divides 5, 6, 129–30, 169
culture change, measuring 153–4
culture of belonging *see* belonging culture
curiosity 114, 117, 146–8, 167
     empowered people 36, 79–80, 82–3
     identity-centred leadership 40–4, 85,
          86, 87

dashboards 155–6
data analysis 61–5, 99, 101
data protection legislation 27
Deloitte 13, 20, 133, 158
demographic data 56, 61, 64
depression 22, 128, 134, 138
deprivation sensitivity 41, 42, 43, 44
development 115–18
disability 9, 20, 78, 112, 115, 116
dismissal 160–1
diversity and inclusion (D&I) xvii, xviii,
          4–20, 68–9, 115
     belonging as key to 3, 6, 21–7
     measurement 89, 155–6
diversity training 118
divided world 4–6
dress codes 20
dynamism, connected teams 47–8, 88

East India Company 11
echo chambers 6, 170
Economist, The 165
education 10, 118, 159
emotional intelligence 138, 139
empathy 36–7, 38, 40, 102–3, 143,
          146, 166
employee lifecycle 111–15
employee resource groups
          (ERGs) 145
empowered people 35–8, 76–83
engagement 55, 56, 154
Equality Act 118
equality vs equity xviii, 84
Eswaran, Vijay 25
ethical fading 34–5
ethnicity 9, 112
exclusion 77, 79
exit process 64, 128, 160–2

facilitators, leaders as *see* identity-centred leadership
feedback 124–6
financial services industry 15, 16
Five Principles of Belonging 29–32, 49–50, 71
  belonging culture 33–5, 75–6
  connected teams 46–9, 87–9
  empowered people 35–8, 76–83
  identity-centred leadership 39–46, 84–5
  organisations and teams as communities where everyone's included 31–2, 72–5
Floyd, George 4, 9
Frankl, Victor Emil 143
Fuller, Michael 22–3
future of work 11–12

Gallup 126
gender 7, 9, 20, 112
Generation Z (Gen Z) 7, 9, 12
GoDaddy 69–70
Godin, Seth 37
Google Dashboard 155
graduate recruitment 159
group-think 17, 24, 81

Hamel, Gary 172
'Harvey Weinstein effect' 16
hate crimes 4
helping employees to thrive *see* thriving
hidden differences xxi–xxii, 9, 17
hierarchy 77, 80, 81, 170, 172
Higgins, John 139
humanity, identity-centred leadership 45–6, 86, 87
hybrid working 171

IBM 141
identity 6–11, 19–20, 21, 114, 145, 167
identity-centred leadership 39–46, 80, 84–6, 140
ignored instances of exclusion 16–17
in-groups 5
Incels 5
inclusive language 112, 116, 118

individual bonuses, scrapping 124
integrity 34–5, 75, 76
internships 113
intersectionality xx, 7, 8, 112, 118
introverts 38, 78, 147
investors 153
Ipsos 165
isolation, and virtual working 137

job descriptions 112
Joy List 146
joyous exploration 41, 42, 43, 44

Kashdan, Todd B. 41
key performance indicators (KPIs) 89
Kopoulos, Ari 46

Lathrap, Mary T., *Judge Softly* 36
leadership 81, 82, 117–18, 124, 127
  see also identity-centred leadership
learning 115–16, 118
Levinson, Harry 160
LGBTQ+ networks 145
LinkedIn 38
local charities, supporting 159–60
local communities, partnering with 159
local education providers, partnering with 159
London Stock Exchange Group 115–16
loneliness 22, 137, 145, 161, 165

male supremacists 5
Martin, Liam McIvor 136
McKinsey 13, 20
meaning, thriving through 143–4
measuring 152–6
media echo chambers 6, 170
mental health 18, 22, 128, 138, 140, 143, 161, 165
  stigma xxi–xxii, 134
  and virtual working 136, 137
mentoring 119–23
meritocracy 5
#MeToo campaign 5
micro-aggressions 5, 77, 118, 140–1
micro-moves 142

Millennials 7, 9, 12, 170
mindfulness 147

narrative arc 99–100
nationalism 5
networks 106, 145
neurodiversity xx–xxi, 78, 115, 118, 160
npower 18
nudge emails 117

office space 171
onboarding processes 38, 114–15
open-mindedness 36–8, 80–3, 85, 114
organisation-community *see* communities,
    organisations and teams as
organisational buy-in 93
   business case, building a robust 94–6
   pitch presentation, creating a 98–104
   sponsorship, advocacy and stakeholders
     104–6
   value proposition, creating your 96–8
Osunsade, Abadesi 74–5, 128–9
Othering and Belonging Institute 173
out-groups 5

parental status 10
People of Color in Tech 129
perception gap 23–7
performance data 64
performance management 123–8
performance-related pay 124
performance reviews 126
person specifications 112–13
personality psychometrics 78
Pettigrew, Andrew 153
physical disability *see* disability
physical qualities 9
pitch presentation 94, 96, 98–104
plan *see* Belonging Plan
Plato 40
polarisation 4–6, 129–30, 169
political rhetoric 4, 6
post-traumatic stress disorder (PTSD) 128
power-interest model 105
power structures 77
privilege 142

process reviews 111
psychometrics 78
pulse surveys 108, 155
purpose 47, 135–6, 143–4

race 9
racism 5, 9, 16, 23, 141–3
Rasca, Andrea 158
recruitment 64, 78, 111–13, 116, 130,
    142, 159
redundancy 162
regional groups and networks 106
regional teams 106
Reitz, Megan 139
Rejection Sensitive Dysphoria 138–9
religion 9
remote working *see* virtual working
resignation 161
retirement 161–2
Return of Kings 5
reverse mentoring 119, 122–3
Richardson, Jillian 146
Rock, David 125
Rodger, Elliot 5
Rooyen, Edwyn van 134

SCARF model 125
scholarships 113
ScienceDaily 170
self-acceptance 166, 167
self-care 166–9
self-compassion 166–9
self-direction, connected teams 48, 88
self-esteem 21, 138
self-regulation 21
Sewell, Bruce 39
sex 20
sex discrimination 16
sexual orientation/identity 9, 20
shared purpose 47, 135–6
shock factor, in pitch presentation 102–3
Shoukry, Hany 169
silos 40, 79–80
Sinek, Simon 45
Singapore 25
Singer, Judy xxi

social curiosity 41, 42, 43, 44
social media 170
social purpose, increased focus on 172
socio-economic background 10, 112
speak-up culture, encouraging a 139–40
sponsorship 104, 105, 106, 119, 120–2, 145
stakeholders 105, 152
stereotype threat xxii
stigma, mental illness xxi–xxii, 134
stories 99, 101–2, 145–8
stress 22, 41, 43, 44, 128, 134
suicide 165
'survivor's guilt' 162

T-Cup 134
talent, identity-centred leader as facilitator
        of 84
targets 89
technology 11, 12
TED Talks 146
telecommuting *see* virtual working
Telegraph 159
Tenbrunsel, Ann 34
tenure data 64
thrill seeking 41, 43, 44
thriving 131
    anti-racism 141–3
    'calling it out' 140
    collective responsibility for 139–40
    and connecting 144–8
    language 138–9
    through purpose and meaning 143–4
    upstanders 140–1
    in a virtual world 135–7
    well-being 132–4, 139–40
Time Doctor 136
timing, Belonging Audit 54
Timpson 159
tracking tools 136
training 116, 118, 122, 160
transgender 20
transparency, belonging culture 33, 75, 76
Trump, Donald 4
trust 33, 47, 120, 122, 125, 134
    identity-centred leadership 40, 44, 84, 85
Twitter 171

understanding 37, 118
unreported instances of exclusion
        16–17
upstanders 120, 140–1

value proposition 96–8, 103, 152
values, and thriving 144
video-conferencing *see* virtual working
virtual working 11, 12, 32, 39, 72, 80, 132,
        135–7, 171
vision 68–70
Vogl, Charles H. xix, 32
Voice for Men, A 5
voluntary work 158–60, 162

Wadors, Pat 38, 102
Weber, Max 170, 171, 172
Weinstein, Harvey 16
well-being xix, 11, 13–14, 128, 132–4,
        139–40
    exit process 160, 161
    identity-centred leader as facilitator of
        40, 85–6
    perception gap 24
    upstanders 140
    and virtual working 136–7
    'work masks" impact on 19–20
    your 168–9
    see also thriving
wellness xix, 40, 85–6
WeWork 171
white supremacists 4
Wipro BPO 114
work experience schemes 159
'work masks' 19–20
workplace, future evolution of the
        170–2
'Workplace Diversity, Inclusion, and
        Intersectionality' survey 16
World Economic Forum 11–12
World Health Organization 165

YouTube 108

Zanini, Michele 172
Zappos 172